Adam Welch

**The Authorship of the Epistle to the Hebrews and Other Papers**

Adam Welch

**The Authorship of the Epistle to the Hebrews and Other Papers**

ISBN/EAN: 9783337316938

Printed in Europe, USA, Canada, Australia, Japan

Cover: Foto ©ninafisch / pixelio.de

More available books at **www.hansebooks.com**

# The Authorship
of the
Epistle to the Hebrews
*And other Papers*

# The Authorship
## of the
# Epistle to the Hebrews
### And other Papers

By
## The Rev. A. Welch
*Minister Emeritus*
Whitevale United Presbyterian Church, Glasgow

"Wee are often constrained to stand alone against the strength of opinion, and to meet the Goliah and Gyant of Authority with contemptible pibbles, and feeble arguments, drawne from the scrip and slender stocke of our selves."
BROWNE'S *Pseudodoxia Epidemica.*

Edinburgh & London
Oliphant Anderson & Ferrier
1898

# PREFACE

THE aim of the following pages is to rescue from error some important questions of scriptural interpretation. The opinions expressed have not been hastily formed. The subject of Melchizedek, for example, has been before the writer's mind, more or less, for over forty years. The elucidation of what the author of Hebrews says on this subject has been with him, during that period, an almost engrossing passion. He has read extensively upon it; and he can say much of that reading was weary, profitless work,—parrot-like repetition in most cases,—but he was anxious to catch any hint that might help him in his task. He does not think that the words of the author of Hebrews are encompassed with any insuperable difficulty, if they are approached in a right spirit. The difficulty which is felt in connexion with them is very much the outcome of a false method of exposition. One of the plainest and most natural canons of interpretation is, that we must take words in their ordinary sense, unless the writer indicates that he uses them otherwise. The author of Hebrews nowhere hints that he uses words about Melchizedek in an unusual sense. But this simple canon has not been followed. It has been assumed that words, in this case, are employed in some tropical or unusual sense, and laborious efforts have been made to show what this sense is. This initial error has also led to the belief that the laws of syntax and logic cannot be applied here; and so there have been ascribed to the sacred penman sentiments which are enough to make him rise from his grave in protest. We believe we have pointed out a better way, though of that our readers must judge.

The author has to record his sincere obligations to Francis T. Barrett, Esq., of the Mitchell Library, Glasgow, and his able assistants, for unfailing courtesy and readiness to help him to find the books which he wished to consult; to the Rev. James Kennedy, B.D., of the New College, Edinburgh, for useful practical advice; and to James Browning, Esq., LL.D., for his kindness in going over the proof sheets.

A. WELCH.

4 Hermitage Terrace,
    Morningside, Edinburgh.

# CONTENTS

| | PAGE |
|---|---|
| I. THE AUTHORSHIP OF HEBREWS . . . . . | 1 |
| II. MELCHIZEDEK: HIS PRIESTHOOD AND PERSONALITY— | |
|     PART I. . . . . . . . . . | 34 |
|     PART II. . . . . . . . . | 52 |
|     PART III. . . . . . . . . | 69 |
| III. CHRIST'S OBJECT IN PREACHING TO THE SPIRITS IN PRISON . . . . . . . . . | 89 |
| IV. THE SIGNIFICANCE OF BAPTISM IN RELATION TO OUR SALVATION . . . . . . . | 144 |
| V. BELIEVERS DEAD TO SIN, BUT RAISED TO LIFE WITH CHRIST . . . . . . . . . | 158 |
| VI. THINGS WHICH MAKE SALVATION CERTAIN . . . | 177 |
| VII. OUR LORD TROUBLED AND TRIUMPHANT . . . | 184 |
| VIII. THE GETHSEMANE CUP: WHAT WAS IT? . . . | 194 |
| IX. IS THE LAST CLAUSE OF JOHN III. 13 GENUINE? . | 201 |

# I

## WHO WAS THE AUTHOR OF THE EPISTLE TO THE HEBREWS?

No one has been able hitherto to answer this question with convincing success. Many, baffled in the attempt, have settled down into the view, long ago expressed by Origen, that the actual truth is, and can be, known only to God. Jerome thought the question of no importance, since the writer was evidently an influential ecclesiastic. This feeling is largely shared in these days. The canonicity of the Epistle is unquestioned, but its authorship is believed to be undiscoverable.[1] To some minds, no doubt, such an attitude is quite satisfactory, but there are others to whom it is far from being so. They remember that canonicity and apostolicity were always closely associated together in the opinion of the early Church. They recall the fact that the Gospels of Mark and Luke were accepted as canonical, mainly, if not entirely, because they were understood to proceed practically from Peter and Paul, and to have had their imprimatur.

We believe that the persistent and laborious efforts which have been made from time to time to settle this much vexed question, which we have undertaken to

[1] *An Introduction to the N. T.*, by Marcus Dods, D.D., p. 177.

discuss, have had their origin in the deep-rooted conviction that the early Church was right in its view of what was necessary to invest any book, put forward as Scripture, with canonical authority. It would be most unjust to ascribe these efforts to mere idle curiosity. Underlying them all there is evidently the conviction that the settlement of this question would greatly strengthen the faith of not a few. We readily admit that there are many, perhaps ninety-nine out of every hundred of the ordinary members of the Christian Church, who do not require any such aid to their faith. Their Christian instinct leads them to feel that the Epistle to the Hebrews has come forth from the heart of God, whoever the actual penman may have been, and with this they are satisfied. They can hardly understand why any one should wish for more. The present writer has been constrained to investigate the question, because he profoundly shares the views of the early Christians on the subject of canonicity.

That those to whom the Epistle was addressed knew the author, at least by name and reputation, is indisputable.[1] This knowledge seems, however, to have been soon lost to the Church from some cause or other. In the early Christian centuries we find critics as much divided in opinion on the question of authorship as they are now. Alford very justly says that we are left, "unfettered by any overpowering judgment of antiquity, to examine the Epistle for ourselves, and form our own opinion from its contents."[2] This, as matter of fact, is what all critics now do.

It would be tedious in the extreme to attempt anything like a review of the different opinions which have been promulgated on the question. There are,

[1] Heb. xiii. 19.     [2] Prolegomena, ch. i. 36, § I.

however, two which seem to us to deserve a few words of remark, if for no other reason, because of the eminence of the men who have held them.

I. The opinion that the author was the Apostle Paul. This has met with much favour both in ancient and modern times. The arguments in support of this view are mainly these—

1. The Epistle was often quoted by the early Christians as the production of the Apostle of the Gentiles. Thus Eusebius, in his Commentary on the Psalms, cites it as the work of *the Apostle*—of *the holy Apostle*—or, of *the divine Apostle*. But this is not to be wondered at in the circumstances, and can hardly be looked upon as of any critical weight. When the author's name had been lost, what more natural than that Paul, who stood so prominently forth then as now, should have been thought to have written it? Apostolic authority seems to be stamped on every verse which it contains. Most people will therefore feel that this view was not unnatural in those early days.

2. The Epistle contains many words and expressions found in Paul's unquestioned writings. But such an argument does not, after all, amount to much. While such words and expressions occur, there are others which are quite foreign to Paul's style, as has been again and again forcibly pointed out in the course of the controversy on the question. In fact, the whole cast of the Epistle is un-Pauline. The argument in favour of the Pauline authorship is usually carried on in a very one-sided way. The expressions and words which seem to coincide with this view are emphasised, while those which are inconsistent with it are ignored. We have a remarkable example of this in

the work of the Rev. Charles Forster, B.D.[1] Let any one, with his eyes open, read over this writer's ponderous volume, and we venture to think its one-sidedness will cure him of all confidence in the belief that Paul was the author of Hebrews.

But, speaking of this argument drawn from the use of certain words and expressions, what more natural than that men, taught by the same Spirit, and writing in the same tongue on the same themes, should use many of the same words and expressions? Would it not be strange if it were otherwise? We venture to assert that any one, taking the trouble to compare what has been written by Dean Farrar and some other like-minded writer on the subject of *the wider hope*, will find many words and phrases, as well as arguments, common to both. But would these coincidences be any proof that both productions were from the same pen? The argument in question is no doubt useful, within certain limits, but many who have used it have certainly ridden it to death. Their conduct irresistibly reminds us of the man who had a house to sell, and who took a brick in his pocket for the satisfaction of possible purchasers. Style is a far deeper and more subtle thing than such an argument implies. It is felt rather than measured. And all competent judges of style say that it is simply impossible to believe in the Pauline authorship of Hebrews.

But the argument which is best fitted to tell against the idea of Pauline authorship is drawn from the words: "How shall we escape, if we neglect so great salvation? which having at the first been spoken by the Lord, was confirmed unto us by them that heard."[2] We

---

[1] *The Apostolical Authority of the Epistle to the Hebrews.*
[2] Heb. ii. 3.

shall have occasion to return to this passage again in the course of our discussion, and to show that commentators have hitherto misunderstood it. But meantime we may confidently ask: can any one acquainted with the spirit by which Paul was actuated for a moment believe that such words ever fell from his pen? Putting aside all mention of apostleship, can the author of such words be the same person who wrote —" But I certify you, brethren, that the gospel which was preached of me is not after men. For I neither received it of man, neither was I taught it, but by the revelation of Jesus Christ "[1]—" If ye have heard of the dispensation of the grace of God which is given me to you-ward: how that by revelation He made known unto me the mystery"?[2] If these words are to have their natural meaning, we cannot see how the Pauline authorship of Hebrews can be maintained.

II. The opinion that the author was Apollos. This view, first suggested by Luther, meets with much favour in the present day. It is supported with much ingenuity and ability by Alford in his valuable Prolegomena to the Epistle. It rests, however, on mere conjecture; and mere conjecture in a case of this kind can never be satisfactory. It is true that Apollos is called "an eloquent man, and mighty in the Scriptures,"[3] but we do not possess a particle of evidence to show that he ever wrote anything. Westcott calls the writer Paul's "fellow apostle," and "The unknown apostle to whom we owe the Epistle to the Hebrews."[4] If these words be well founded, Apollos is simply ruled out of court.

As the other views which have been propounded

---

[1] Gal. i. 11, 12.     [2] Eph. iii. 2.     [3] Acts xviii. 24.
[4] Introduction to his *Epistle to the Hebrews*, p. lii.

rest on no better foundation, we cannot stay to discuss them.

The date of the Epistle is closely bound up with the question of its authorship. On this subject Alford says, "Almost all commentators agree in believing that our Epistle was written *before the destruction of Jerusalem*" (A.D. 70). Lünemann uses these words: "That supposition is thus the most natural one which places the date of the Epistle's composition between the years 65 and 67."[1] Westcott arrives at very much the same conclusion when he says, "The letter may be placed in the critical interval between A.D. 64, the government of Gossius Florus, and 67, the commencement of the Jewish War, and most probably just before the breaking of the storm in the latter year."[2] Any one of these dates, even the latest, is definite enough for the purposes of our present argument. Let us accept, then, the year 70.

This date—indeed any date usually given—has a distinct bearing on the interpretation of the words in ch. ii. 3 to which we have already referred, as will immediately appear. To make this apparent it will be necessary to quote the passage again, "How shall we escape, if we neglect so great salvation; which, having at the first been spoken (ἀρχὴν λαβοῦσα λαλεῖσθαι) by the Lord, was confirmed unto us by them that heard (ὑπὸ τῶν ἀκουσάντων εἰς ἡμᾶς ἐβεβαιώθη). Lünemann, referring to this passage, says, "Here the author reckons himself among the number of those who have received their knowledge of the gospel, not immediately from the Lord Himself, but only through the medium of the first disciples and ear-

---

[1] Introduction to his *Handbook to Hebrews* (Eng. tr.), pp. 63, 64.
[2] Introduction to his *Epistle to the Hebrews*, p. xlii.

witnesses. He claims thus no equal rank with the twelve apostles, but takes his place at the standpoint of Luke (Luke i. 2).[1] Alford is equally explicit, "The author was *not an apostle*, nor in the strictest sense a contemporary of the apostles, so that he should have seen and heard our Lord for himself. He belongs to the second rank, in point of time, of apostolic men,—to those who heard from eye- and ear-witnesses. This will follow from the consideration of the passage ch. ii. 3."[2] Dr. William Lindsay expresses the same view of the verse when he says, "The meaning undoubtedly is, that the truth first received from the lips of the Saviour was handed down by the apostles safe and entire to posterity."[3] We might quote the views of many other commentators—Westcott, for example—to the same effect. But this is unnecessary. The quotations already made are sufficient to show what is the universal interpretation of the passage in question. On this interpretation we have the following criticisms to offer:—

1. The date generally assigned to the Epistle places its author within the apostolic age. Alford cannot be justified, therefore, in saying that he was not in the strictest sense a contemporary of the apostles. James, the brother of John, was certainly dead, and, most probably, Paul also; but can these deaths be said to terminate the apostolic age? We know that John was now living, and we have no warrant for saying that all the other apostles were in their graves.

2. It is not necessary to suppose that the author identifies himself with his readers when he uses the words, *was confirmed unto us*. He may be referring to

---

[1] Introduction, p. 11.   [2] Alford, Proleg. ch. i. 157, § I.
[3] *Epistle to the Hebrews*, vol. i. p. 87.

himself and others, and not to his readers at all. We shall see by and by that there is force in this criticism.

3. The expression ἀρχὴν λαβοῦσα is interpreted too loosely when it is applied in a general way to our Lord's public ministry. When used in connexion with the origination of the gospel, as it is in the passage under consideration, the word ἀρχήν is strictly confined to the very commencement of its announcement,—" The beginning (ἀρχή, the very commencement) of the gospel of Jesus Christ."[1]  " Even as they delivered them unto us, which from the beginning (ἀπ' ἀρχῆς, from the very commencement) were eye-witnesses and ministers of the word," etc.[2]

4. It is not a natural interpretation of ἐβεβαιώθη to make it mean, as Dr. Lindsay does, *was handed down by the apostles safe and entire to posterity*. Westcott, however, attaches the same meaning to the word— " Was brought unto us—into our midst—and confirmed to us." This is reading a meaning into the term, not expounding it. The word in its different forms always conveys the idea of something which has been in uncertainty but is now established. A few examples may be adduced to illustrate our meaning: " Even as the testimony of Christ was confirmed (ἐβεβαιώθη) in you."[3]  " In the defence and confirmation (βεβαιώσει) of the gospel."[4]  " For men swear by the greater, and in every dispute of theirs the oath is final for confirmation " (εἰς βεβαίωσιν).[5]  In all these three examples something is assumed to be insecure or uncertain, but is afterwards established or made certain. We shall see by and by how this

---

[1] Mark i. 1.     [2] Luke i. 2.     [3] 1 Cor. i. 6.
[4] Phil. i. 7.     [5] Heb. vi. 16.

natural meaning of the word should be given to it in the case in question. But—

5. The words in the fourth verse (which immediately follows that now under notice) cannot be naturally interpreted in accordance with the traditional exposition of the third verse. "God also bearing witness with them, both by signs and wonders, and by manifold powers, and by gifts of the Holy Ghost, according to His own will." Dr. Westcott understands these words as describing what took place in connexion with the gospel in post-apostolic times. His words are: "This passage is of deep interest as showing the unquestioned reality of miraculous gifts in the early Church, and the way in which they were regarded as co-ordinate with other exhibitions of divine power."[1] We believe that this note is founded on an entire misapprehension of the meaning of the sacred penman. Do the inspired writer's words look as if they were a record of what took place in post-apostolic times? Do they not rather read as an account of the signs and wonders wrought by our Lord in attestation of His divine mission? We do not deny that they may refer also to what took place on the day of Pentecost, and to the miraculous manifestations given in connexion with the ministry of the apostles. But to make them apply only to post-apostolic times, as Westcott does, is (we do not hesitate to say it) to misread them. We do not think Church history bears out the assertion that such signs and wonders were wrought in the Church after the days of the apostles.

What, then, do we consider the plain and natural meaning of the two verses which we have been ex-

[1] Westcott, *in loco.*

amining? We answer, with some degree of confidence, this: Our Lord, at the very commencement of His public ministry, spoke to certain persons, evidently a limited number, of the salvation which He came to work out for men. These persons, and some others associated with them, had evidently been entertaining conjectures of this nature about Him. When, therefore, the Lord had unequivocally confirmed these conjectures, those who received this welcome information hastened to convey it to their circle of friends. And thus the truth was established in the minds of all the company. It was more fully established, as time went on, by the miracles and gifts of the Holy Ghost. Does this not seem a more natural interpretation of these two verses than that which is given in the traditional exposition?

But can we point out the time when our Lord first made mention of His great salvation? and can we put our hand upon those to whom this first mention was made? We can. There is a remarkable answer to these questions in the first chapter of the Gospel according to John. We quote the passage in full: "Again on the morrow John was standing, and two of his disciples; and he looked upon Jesus as He walked, and saith, Behold, the Lamb of God! And the two disciples heard him speak, and followed Jesus. And Jesus turned, and beheld them following, and saith unto them, What seek ye? And they said unto Him, Rabbi (which is to say, being interpreted, Master), where abidest Thou? He saith unto them, Come, and ye shall see. They came therefore and saw where He abode; and they abode with Him that day: it was about the tenth hour. One of the two that heard John (εἷς ἐκ τῶν δύο τῶν ἀκουσάντων), and followed him, was Andrew, Simon Peter's brother. He findeth first his own brother Simon, and saith unto him, We have found the Messias (which is, being interpreted, Christ). He brought him unto Jesus. Jesus looked upon him, and said, Thou art Simon the son of John: thou shalt be called Cephas (which is by interpretation, Peter)."[1]

Seldom do we find one passage of Scripture so completely explaining another as the verse in Hebrews (ch. ii. 3), which we are striving to rescue from misconception, explains that in John's Gospel. We are surprised that its explanatory character should hitherto have so entirely eluded the notice of interpreters. The words τῶν ἀκουσάντων, common to both passages, seem to have been beckoning to one another all these centuries to come near and give mutual explanations. Who were the two disciples who heard John the Baptist invite them to behold the Lamb of God? They were Andrew, Simon Peter's brother, and John, the beloved disciple, the author of the Gospel narrative from which the above incident has been extracted, though he modestly omits his name. They were the first to hear from the lips of Jesus the announcement of His great salvation. No doubt they told Him their reason for following and accosting Him,—John the Baptist had on the previous day pointed out Jesus, either to these two disciples or to others, as "the Lamb of God, which taketh away the sin of the world!"[2] But at all events John's words, reaching these two brethren, had excited their curiosity and set them a-thinking, so that on the first opportunity they resolved to make

[1] John i. 35-42.   [2] John i. 39.

the acquaintance of Jesus. They showed by their conduct that a deep interest had been excited in their minds; and they would ask Him what John's words meant. So that Jesus must have been naturally led to speak of Himself as having come into the world to save sinners. Is not this the natural explanation of the words that *the great salvation was first spoken by the Lord*? Andrew, overjoyed at the discovery which he and his associate John had made, hastened to convey the precious news to his brother Peter. The same good news was, no doubt, conveyed to all their godly companions. Is not this the natural explanation of the remark that what Jesus had said *was confirmed* to Peter and his friends by them who heard? The testimony of Jesus was further confirmed by signs and miracles. The ἀκούσαντες of Hebrews and of John's Gospel are one and the same. In John's Gospel prominence is given to what the Baptist said; in Hebrews, to what was said by Christ.

But we get more out of the passage from John's Gospel than the correct exposition of a hitherto misunderstood text in Hebrews. We actually get an answer to the great question which we have undertaken to investigate. It will be observed that in this passage attention is specially directed to Peter. He is made specially prominent as the person to whom, in the first instance, the declaration made by Jesus was conveyed. After the Baptist's first words directing his disciples to Christ as the Lamb of God appointed to take away the sin of the world, Peter would naturally have his doubts and uncertainties. All doubts and uncertainties were removed, and his mind was *confirmed* by what had been told him by his brother Andrew. If, therefore, we are right in our view of the two passages which we have brought together and compared, then we have found the author of Hebrews, not among the successors of the apostles, but within the small circle of our Lord's first disciples. And in this small circle, who could it be but the Apostle of the Circumcision? In fact, the passage in Hebrews, on the elucidation of which we have spent so much pains, if taken in connexion with the quotation made from John's Gospel, points out as distinctly as words can, that in Peter, and in no one else, we are to find the long-lost author of Hebrews!

When we recognise Peter as the author of Hebrews, we feel at once that an inequality which has hitherto existed in our New Testament has been redressed. The Apostle of the Circumcision seems now to have something like his due share of space assigned to him. There may not be much in this, but one can hardly help thinking of it. Does it not seem anomalous that we should have only two small Epistles from the pen of an apostle who occupied so important a position during our Lord's public ministry, and figured so prominently in connexion with the early organisation of the Christian Church? We naturally expect him to have relatively something like the same prominent position in the New Testament that he occupied in the early Church. What a contrast between the space his writings occupy and that assigned to Paul! It is true that the Jews are in a small minority compared with the Gentiles; and we could hardly have expected to find so much notice taken of them in connexion with their apostle as is taken of the Gentiles in connexion with theirs. Still, when we think of the prominence assigned to Peter by our Lord, and of the high place which the Jews had in the divine regards and purposes, we feel that there is some incongruity when only two small Epistles are assigned to the Apostle of the Circumcision. It almost looks as if the Church had conspired to rob Peter of his rights, just because he was the Apostle of the Circumcision, in the same way as, in the dark ages, the Jews were persecuted for the crime committed by their forefathers. Some even grudge him credit for both of the Epistles which bear his name. When we ascribe to him the Epistle to the Hebrews, we feel as if somehow something like justice were done to him. The subjects discussed in that work are just those with which the Apostle of the Circumcision might have been expected to deal. The doctrine of the eternal priesthood of Christ is, especially, such a subject as naturally belongs to him; and it receives full discussion only in the Epistle to the Hebrews.

Support for the conclusion to which our investigations have brought us comes from many quarters. And this support is all the more valuable because in every case it is given unintentionally. The Rev. Ch. Frid. Boehme writes, "It was long ago noticed by New Testament interpreters that no small resemblance of words and formulas exists between our Epistle (Hebrews) and that which is regarded as the first of Peter."[1] Riehm declares that no New Testament writer has such affinity with Peter as the author of the Epistle to the Hebrews.[2] The Rev. A. B. Davidson, LL.D., says, "It is the opinion of many

---

[1] *Epist. ad Hebræos Prefatio*, p. 40.
[2] *Lehrbegriff des Hebräerbriefes*, p. 855.

writers who have bestwowed much attention on the Epistle, that, though the first impression which it produces is, that it strongly resembles the Pauline Epistles, when more fundamentally examined its deeper and real affinities are found to be with the primitive apostolic teaching as exhibited in the early speeches in the Acts, and in the Epistles of Peter and James."[1] The Rev. Charles Foster, B.D., already referred to, says that there is a close resemblance in style between Hebrews and 1 Peter.

None of these writers, however, dream of ascribing to Peter the Epistle to the Hebrews. All seem to think it beyond his capacity. Why, were not all our Lord's apostles, with the exception of Paul, ignorant and uncultured men? Boehme thinks that the First Epistle of Peter was written by Silas. He grounds his opinion on ch. v. 12, when he finds the words, "By Silvanus a faithful brother, as I conceive, I have written unto you briefly." He attaches no importance to the fact that Peter's name stands at the head of the Epistle. He does not believe it possible that Peter, who was a Jew and so long resident in Palestine, could have written such elegant Greek as this Epistle presents. This is a grievous error, as we shall see by and by; but Boehme is not the only one who has been led into it. This writer also institutes a careful comparison between similar phrases and words common to Hebrews and 1 Peter, as if he meant to refute thereby his own conclusion. He finds nearly forty such cases, and some of them are very striking. As, therefore, we cannot set aside the Petrine authorship of 1 Peter, we claim all that Boehme has done to show the affinity between Hebrews and 1 Peter as in

[1] *Bible Handbook to the Epistle to the Hebrews*, p. 32.

favour of the conclusion to which we have been brought.

The bulky volume of the Rev. Charles Forster, B.D., was written to establish the Pauline authorship of Hebrews. The writer thinks that his attempt has been successful. He finds the resemblance between Hebrews and 1 Peter to be so striking that he infers Peter must have borrowed from Paul, that is, from Hebrews, copying many of his words and phrases. With what singular persistency is everything like originality or culture denied to the Apostle of the Circumcision!

Mr. Forster appeals in support of his conclusion to the words, "And account that the long-suffering of our Lord is salvation; even as our beloved brother Paul also, according to the wisdom given to him, wrote unto you; as also in all his Epistles, speaking in them of these things; wherein are some things hard to be understood, which the ignorant and unsteadfast wrest, as they do also the other Scriptures, unto their own destruction."[1] As Paul is mentioned in this passage, Mr. Forster apparently thinks it would greatly help his argument if he could show that Peter's words here point to some passage in Hebrews. And so it would. He refers, at p. 511 of his work, to the following passages in Hebrews to which he thinks Peter's words just quoted undoubtedly refer, namely, chs. vi. 12, iv. 15, 16, ii. 17, 18, and xii. 24. He wishes us to believe that these passages correspond in thought to the words, "The long-suffering of our Lord is salvation." We have carefully examined these passages and—not one of them supports his contention.

There is not in any of Paul's Epistles (and certainly

[1] 2 Pet. iii. 15, 16.

not in Hebrews) such a passage as Peter here refers to, except one, namely, Romans, "Or despisest thou the riches of His goodness and forbearance and long-suffering, not knowing that the goodness of God leadeth thee to repentance?"[1] The Rev. J. R. Lumby, D.D., who writes the exposition of 2 Peter in the *Speaker's Commentary*, says on ch. iii. 15, "The passage in the writings of St. Paul which comes nearest to the language of this verse is Rom. ii. 4, which Epistle being written to the Jewish as well as to the Gentile converts at Rome." We can get over Peter's reference, if it is not to this passage in Romans, only by saying that it must point to some passage in some letter that has now been lost. But neither will that supposition help Mr. Forster.

The most effective support for our conclusion comes from the Rev. Frederick Rendall, A.M. And this support is all the more valuable that he never dreams of Peter as the author of Hebrews, but infers that the writer must be either a personal disciple of his, or a diligent student of his Epistle. He says, "Comparison of the First Epistle of Peter reveals to us a closer sympathy between our author and that apostle than that which we have noted with the other great Apostle of the Circumcision" (James).[2] Further, "Again and again we find in St. Peter's Epistle the germ of the author's thought, or the exact form of expression."[3] The following comparisons between the two Epistles are taken exclusively from Mr. Rendall's work:—

Both regard the Christian *hope*[4] and Christian *salvation*[5] as objective realities, and an eventful future

---

[1] Rom. ii. 4.    [2] *Theology of the Hebrew Christians*, p. 42.
[3] *Ibid.* p. 43.    [4] 1 Pet. i. 3 and Heb. vi. 18.
[5] 1 Pet. i. 5-10 and Heb. i. 14, ix. 28.

inheritance reserved till the second coming of Christ.

Both regard *faith* as steadfast trust in an unseen God which sustains His servants under temptation, and secures them final inheritance of His promises.[1]

Both regard righteousness as an upright life.[2]

Both emphatically connect the sufferings of Christ with our future glory as two co-ordinate parts of God's scheme of redemption.[3]

Both give the same prominence to Christ's fellowship with us in suffering, and to the value of suffering as a necessary discipline.[4]

Both—and they are alone in this—make emphatic mention of *the blood of sprinkling*.[5]

Both—and in this also they are alone—designate the Lord as the *Shepherd*.[6]

Both call Christ *Captain*. Here, however, Hebrews is compared with Peter's words in the Acts, not in the Epistle.[7]

Both—and they are alone in this also—insist on our privileges as members of *the house of God*.[8]

Both connect the possession of a good conscience with good habits of life.[9]

Both—and in this also they are alone—mention the blessing pronounced by the ninth beatitude on those who suffer for Christ's sake.[10]

---

[1] 1 Pet. i. 5–9, v. 9 and Heb. xi. 1.
[2] 1 Pet. ii. 24, iii. 14; Heb. vi. 10, x. 23, 24, xii. 1–3, 14.
[3] 1 Pet. i. 11 and Heb. ii. 10.
[4] 1 Pet. ii. 19–23, iv. 1, 13, and Heb. ii. 10–18, v. 7, 8, xii. 2–8.
[5] 1 Pet. i. 2 and Heb. xii. 24.
[6] 1 Pet. ii. 25, v. 3, and Heb. xiii. 20.
[7] Acts iii. 15, v. 31; Heb. ii. 10, xii. 2.
[8] 1 Pet. ii. 5 and Heb. iii. 6.
[9] 1 Pet. iii. 16 and Heb. xiii. 18.
[10] 1 Pet. iv. 14 and Heb. xi. 26.

Both Epistles end with a similar form of blessing.[1]

Both Epistles are singular in having the expressions ἐπ' ἐσχάτου, λόγος ζῶν, ἀναφέρειν ἁμαρτίας, θυσίας ἀναφέρειν, ἀντίτυπος, ἔννοια.[2]

After having called attention to such striking facts as these, one's only wonder is, that Mr. Rendall was unable to draw the only conclusion to which they point.

We come now to the question of Peter's ability to write such a treatise as the Epistle to the Hebrews. It has too long been the custom to represent our Lord's apostles in general as rude, ignorant, illiterate men, and to speak of Paul as the only theologian of the Christian faith, and the sole possessor of literary attainments. We can to some extent sympathise with the feeling which underlies this representation,— the desire to magnify the grace of God in enabling men of this stamp to accomplish such a spiritual revolution in the world,—but it is a foul calumny, all the same, whatever the motive which dictated it may have been. It is not for us to measure the potency of God's grace: we at once admit that God might have used illiterate men to carry out His gracious purposes. He might have employed them as mere machines for the purpose of expressing His will through them, though on such a supposition it does not appear impossible to believe that He might for this purpose have enabled Peter to write in the cultured style which Hebrews exhibits. But—and the remark is a trite one—He does not work miracles unnecessarily. A good reason may be given why the disciples were used as automata on the day of

[1] 1 Pet. v. 10, 11 and Heb. xiii. 20-22.
[2] *Theology of the Hebrew Christians*, pp. 43-45.

Pentecost; but the case is quite different when we come to contemplate the apostles as men appointed to carry the gospel to the ends of the earth.

The habit of regarding our Lord's apostles generally as rude and unlettered men is, in large measure, due to a misunderstanding of a passage in the narrative in Acts iv. The words run thus: "Now when they (the ecclesiastical authorities at Jerusalem before whom Peter and John had been brought) beheld the boldness of Peter and John, and had perceived that they were unlearned and ignorant men, they marvelled; and they took knowledge of them that they had been with Jesus." Now, the fact that these brethren awakened astonishment by the way in which they spoke hardly consists with the idea that they were ignorant and unlearned. The marvel was that they were the very reverse. They spoke with a wisdom and power which called forth the reluctant admiration of their enemies. The wonder could be explained only by the conviction that they had received their instruction from Christ. For the teaching of Christ had struck all as possessed of commanding wisdom. Peter and John had evidently received a portion of his Spirit. And certainly they were *ignorant and unlearned* only in the sense of making no use of rabbinical formulas and illustrations. Their style of speech was independent, through the liberty wherewith Christ makes His people free. They were not trammelled by traditional forms.

But what we wish to call special attention to here is the fact that the name of John is most closely associated with that of Peter in this narrative, though Peter figures as the principal speaker. There is not the slightest hint that Peter was regarded as inferior in culture to John. The two are put together in the same category. Now, modern scholars are ready to admit the culture and literary ability of the author of the Fourth Gospel. They place him, in this respect, on a platform very much higher than that on which the Apostle of the Gentiles stands. It is to insult him to describe him as an unlettered fisherman. Peter seems to have been, socially and otherwise, very much on a par with him. They both belonged to the same locality. If, then, John could obtain a scholarly education in his native place, why might not Peter also?

Let us now turn to the New Testament to see if we can discover whether Peter is correctly described when he is spoken of as *unlettered*. He comes before us on several occasions in the Acts, and always as a man possessed of singular mental alertness and profound acquaintance with Scripture. He is always ready to make use of his knowledge in a way admirably suited to the circumstances. Then, take his First Epistle, or even his Second,—and we see no good reason for rejecting it,—is there any proof in these of his unfitness for writing the Epistle to the Hebrews? Peter, with his fellow-apostles of Galilee, has long been spoken of as illiterate without any warrant whatever. Peter and John were certainly not illiterate.

But, further, this estimate of Peter, apart altogether from the positive evidence which we possess in opposition to it, is totally inconsistent with all reasonable probabilities. God has taught the modern Church that it is vain to send into the foreign field any but our ablest and best trained men. There was as much need for such men in primitive times as now. Are we to believe that our Lord, in sending forth the apostles, acted in a total different spirit from that which He inculcates on us? The idea is inconceivable. We must, then, dismiss from our minds all thought of Peter's inability to write that treatise of which we have, we think, produced sufficient grounds for believing him to have been the author. To our mind it is plain that Peter, in the providence of God, was prepared for the work which he had to do as certainly as was the Apostle of the Gentiles. He had a subtle race to deal with in his kinsmen, and he was chosen by our Lord for the work of propagating the gospel among them, because, by natural endowments and intellectual training, he was admirably fitted for the task. And his Epistle to the Hebrews, if we are right in ascribing it to him, as we do not now hesitate to believe, entitles him to occupy no second place when we speak of New Testament theologians.

We have thus finished the task we assigned to ourselves, and might now lay down our pen. There are, however, *three* subordinate inquiries, usually associated with the main question, which must not be ignored.

1. To whom was the Epistle sent? The answer to this question does not seem to be attended with insuperable difficulty, if we are willing to deal fairly with the available facts. The passage on which we mainly build is 2 Pet. iii. 15, "And account that the long-suffering of our Lord is salvation; even as our beloved brother Paul also, according to the wisdom given to him, wrote to you ($\dot{v}\mu\hat{\imath}\nu$)." We have seen that nowhere in Paul's Epistles, and certainly not in Hebrews, is any passage to be found that can be regarded as here referred to by Peter, if we except Rom. ii. 4. That the Epistle in which was the

passage pointed to by Peter has been lost, is too violent a supposition to be seriously entertained. To take refuge in such a theory would be too much like a wilful closing of one's eyes to the light. We think, therefore, that Peter's words justify the conclusion that both the Epistle to the Romans and the Second Epistle of Peter were addressed to Christians at Rome. The former was, of course, meant for Gentiles as well as Jews. The latter, however, bears on the face of it that it was intended for the Jewish section of the Church only. This is a most important conclusion to have reached. Indeed, it is of vital moment in connexion with the question now under discussion. Let us keep it firmly before our minds..

From this vantage ground we are able to advance another step. In 2 Pet. iii. 1 occur the words, "This is now, beloved, the *second* Epistle that I write unto you." That is to say, what we now call Peter's Second Epistle is his *second* to the Jewish Christians at Rome. This is a somewhat startling conclusion, but it seems impossible to escape from it. What we call the First and Second Epistles of Peter do not seem to have been intended for the same circle of readers. The *First* Epistle is addressed to "the sojourners of the Dispersion in Pontus, Galatia," etc.; the *Second*, "to them that have obtained like precious faith with us in the righteousness of our God and Saviour Jesus Christ." These inscriptions are so different that they naturally suggest that the Epistles could not have been intended for the same class of readers. This suggestion is confirmed by an examination of the contents of the Epistles.

The whole tone of *First* Peter is different from that of *Second*. The *First* is more hortatory, the *Second* more admonitory. When writing his *Second* Epistle the apostle evidently felt the need of putting forth every possible effort to keep his readers in the right way. He feels that the circle of readers to whom that Epistle was addressed were more in danger of falling away than those to whom his First Epistle was sent. In short, he seems to have in his mind just such a community as is pointed to in Hebrews. The Judæo-Christians at Rome were just such a community as both Epistles indicate. The Jewish Christians at Rome were in special danger of apostatising. The excitement produced there by the introduction of Christianity placed them in a very trying position. We may well believe that they were often tempted to waver in their faith, and to ask themselves the question, whether the hostility excited against them was not a punishment sent upon them for forsaking their ancestral faith.

The early coming of Christ to rescue His people from all the evils of their present condition was a strong hope in the primitive Church. The delay of this coming appears to have relaxed the faith of many. There were scoffers who said, "Where is the promise of His coming? For, from the day that the fathers fell asleep, all things continue as they were from the beginning of the creation." This is so like the state of things indicated in Hebrews that we have been constrained to conclude that both Epistles, that is, Hebrews and Second Peter, were addressed to the Jewish section of the Church at Rome. The inscription of *Second* Peter seems to accord well with this idea. Just as there is no direct indication of the parties to whom Hebrews was addressed, so there is none in 2 Peter in the words, "them that have obtained like precious faith with us in the righteousness of our God and Saviour Jesus Christ." And the same reason, or reasons, which operated in leaving the destination of Hebrews indefinite, may well have operated also in connexion with Peter's *Second* Epistle. To this point we shall return again by and by; but meanwhile, in view of what has been said, we believe the three Epistles with which we have been dealing should be classified otherwise than at present in the New Testament. We would arrange them thus—

(1) The Epistle of Peter to the converted Jews of the Dispersion (1 Peter).

(2) The First Epistle of Peter to the converted Jews at Rome (Epistle to the Hebrews).

(3) The Second Epistle of Peter to the converted Jews at Rome (2 Peter).

The Epistle which we have placed first in this list has all the appearance of a circular letter. If what we call the *Second* Epistle of Peter had been addressed to the same persons designated in the *First*, it is strange that it was not inscribed in the same way.

In support of the conclusion that the Epistle to the Hebrews was addressed to the Judæo-Christians at Rome is the strong evidence of ch. xiii. 24, "They of (ἀπό) Italy salute you," literally, "They from Italy," etc. The idea is that these brethren belonged to Italy but were now resident elsewhere, and in the locality from which Peter was now writing. We find in the New Testament many examples of the same use of the preposition ἀπό. "Jesus from (ἀπό) Nazareth of Galilee." "Then there came to Jesus from (ἀπό) Jerusalem Pharisees and scribes." "And certain of them from (ἀπό) Cilicia and Asia." "And certain of the brethren from (ἀπό) Joppa." In all these passages the idea is that the persons spoken of were at the time away from the places to which they belonged. The Italians, whose salutations Peter sent to his readers, were at the time out of their own country for some reason or other, possibly in the pursuit of business, or because of the persecution to which they had been exposed in the Eternal City. Now, what more likely than that Christian Jews living out of Italy should wish to send a kindly message to their Christian kinsmen at Rome?

That the Epistle was intended for the Christian Jews at Rome is further supported by what we know of its history. Our earliest notices of it are connected with Rome. Clement, one of the earliest pastors of the Church there, and who is generally believed to have been the same Clement mentioned in Phil. iv. 3 as one of Paul's fellow-workers, manifests in his Epistle to the Corinthians (as the Epistle sent by the Church at Rome to the Church at Corinth is usually called) a minute acquaintance with it.[1] Dr. William Kay, in the *Speaker's Commentary*, tells us that Clement of Rome, who wrote towards the end of the first century, says, according to Eusebius, "He not only borrows many thoughts from the Epistle to the Hebrews, but uses its very words."[2] He adds, "It is certain, then, that before the end of the first century this Epistle was held in the highest honour by the Roman Church, and was used with at least as much deference as was accorded to Epistles of confessedly

---

[1] Reuss, *Hist. of Christ. Theol. in the Apost. Age*, says Clement "frequently and very directly copies passages from the Epistle to the Hebrews. Thus ch. xxxvi. is composed almost entirely of extracts from that Epistle."—Eng. tr. vol. ii. p. 289.

[2] *E. H.* iii. 38.

apostolic origin."[1] It was the most natural thing in the world that the pastor of a Church which had received such an Epistle should be well acquainted with its contents, and should display that acquaintance in an Epistle which he is generally credited with having written.

2. Was Peter personally acquainted with his readers? and had he been at Rome before this Epistle was written? Nothing can be inferred from the fact that no persons are specially named as having had salutations sent to them. The same reason or reasons which induced him to refrain from inserting his name in the body of the Epistle may have operated to keep him from mentioning the names of others. The question now under consideration turns very much on the precise meaning which we attach to the word ἀποκατασταθῶ in ch. xiii. 19, and which our translators render *may be restored*. " Pray for us, for we are persuaded that we have a good conscience, desiring to live honestly in all things. And I exhort you the more exceedingly to do this that I may be restored to you the sooner." If that rendering be accepted and taken in its full natural sense, then we are compelled to say Peter must have been at Rome before this Epistle was written.

Dr. A. B. Davidson says,[2] " These words imply a former residence of the writer among the Hebrews. He contemplated a return to them, a return desired by himself, and one which he assumes will be acceptable to them—and he beseeches them to help it by their prayers." Dr. Vaughan says,[3] " The writer

---
[1] *Introduction to Epistle to the Hebrews*, p. 2.
[2] *Bible Handbook to Hebrews, in loco.*
[3] *Epistle to the Hebrews, in loco.*

stood in some established relation to them, at least of acquaintance and intercourse, if not of pastoral supervision."

But, is it quite certain that the rendering of our translators, which these scholars follow, fairly brings out Peter's meaning? Etymologically the word ἀποκαθίστημι merely conveys the idea of the transference of a person or thing from one place to another, or from one state to another. Thus, in the case before us, the meaning seems simply to be that Peter earnestly solicited the prayers of his readers that he might be brought to them speedily. There was evidently something, apparently Timothy's absence, which stood in the way, and his request was that they should pray God to remove the impediment.

Lexicologists refer us for the interpretation of the word to Polybius. And in that author, as elsewhere, the word no doubt means *restore*. But, instead of going to Polybius for the meaning of this word, would it not be more natural to apply to the LXX.? Interpreters have pointed out again and again that the writer of Hebrews uniformly relies on that venerable translation. Now, the LXX. do not, by any means, limit the meaning of the word to the sense assigned to it by our translators. They use it in at least *ten* different senses.

Nor is it indisputable that *restore* is always its meaning in the New Testament. The word occurs in Matt. xvii. 11: "And he answered and said, Elijah indeed cometh, and shall restore (ἀποκαταστήσει) all things." Now, our contention is that the simple etymological meaning is the proper sense here. We do not need, of course, to say that our Lord by Elijah here means *John the Baptist*. It is impossible for us to believe that John the Baptist brought all things back to the condition in which they had formerly been. Does the narrative of his ministry, given us by the evangelists, convey any such idea? Cremer in his Lexicon, *sub voce*, makes an earnest attempt to bring out of the passage the full idea conveyed by the word *restore*. He sets aside several methods which have been suggested for securing this result, and at last finds rest in the thought that John restored the operation of the Old Covenant! What this means, we confess we do not quite understand. Does he mean to affirm that John by his ministry, in any actual sense, re-established a state of things such as ever previously existed among God's ancient people? If so, then he affirms as fact what never happened. What John actually did was to prepare for Christ. He was the Lord's herald—as he himself declared— "the voice of one crying in the wilderness, Make ye ready the way of the Lord, make His paths straight." His ministry introduced that of Christ. It was through John's instrumentality that our Lord's first disciples were secured. He laid the train which led to the establishment of Christianity. Arguing from this instance of the use of the word under consideration, it seems to us that all that Peter means in the verse, the right meaning of which we are seeking to establish, is that he hoped in answer to the prayers of his readers he might be permitted to come and see them, without its being implied that he had ever been with them before. His wish was to be brought to them—introduced to them.

Then there is that passage in the first chapter of the Acts. Just before our Lord's ascension His disciples asked Him the question, "Lord, doest Thou at this time *restore* (ἀποκαθιστάνεις) the kingdom to Israel?" Here we are met with the same difficulty as we encountered in connexion with the passage in Matthew. What was to be restored? Was it the dominion which Israel had at one time enjoyed? That cannot be the meaning. The old kingdom was not to be set up again. The kingdom of Christ is of a totally different character. No one can escape from this criticism by saying that the disciples misunderstood the nature of the new kingdom. Our Lord, who replied to their question, gives no hint that this was the case. It seems to us that the sense here is, "Dost Thou at this time *introduce* or *convey* the kingdom back to Israel?"

We have made these remarks simply in the interests of sound exposition. We hold no brief from the Church of Rome in favour of their tradition that Peter was for twenty-five years bishop of the Church in the Eternal City. Our argument does not depend upon the question whether Peter was ever actually in Rome. It is, however, a persistent tradition that Peter was for some time head of the Church in the Roman capital. What is stated in Hebrews is not sufficient to confirm this tradition. It may all have arisen out of Peter's expressed wish to visit the brethren there. We know how legends of this kind grow.

The words in ch. xiii. 23 seem most in harmony with the idea that Peter, when he wrote his Epistle, had no personal acquaintance with his readers. "Ye know that Timothy hath been set at liberty" (ἀπολελυμένον), or, as some render the word, "hath been sent away: with whom, if he come shortly, I will see you." Peter seems here to lean upon Timothy for some reason or other. Is not the natural inference that this was because Timothy was personally known to the brethren at Rome, while Peter was not? Should Timothy be able to accompany Peter on his proposed journey, he would greatly help his influence with the brethren in the Eternal City. If Peter needed a personal introduction to the Christians there, Timothy could give it to him. We think, therefore, we see a beautiful modesty in Peter's thus leaning on Paul's companion. He seems to desire to do nothing, and to say nothing, that might affect the place which Paul had in the affections of the Church at Rome. We are taking it for granted that Paul was dead at this time. Westcott says Paul was martyred in the year A.D. 65.[1] And Dr. A. B. Davidson says, "The Epistle must have been written some time, and it is usually thought only a very few years, after the Neronic persecution,"[2] which began in the year A.D. 64.

After Paul's decease, if doctrinal disputes or difficulties arose among the Jewish converts at Rome, what more natural than that Peter should be applied to? He must by this time have been well known throughout the Church as the Apostle of the Circumcision. He would therefore be looked upon as the proper person to guide them now that Paul was no more. We believe that he was thus appealed to, and that this appeal accounts for the origin of the Epistle.

3. Why did Peter not append his name to this Epistle if, as we believe, he wrote it? And why did he not specify the readers for whom it was meant? Several answers may be given to these queries.

(*a*) He may have had a shyness in putting his name

---

[1] Introduction to *Hebrews*, p. 42.
[2] Introduction to *Bible Handbook to Hebrews*.

to the Epistle, considering what Paul had been to his readers. He may have wished to rely entirely on the arguments which he could adduce from Scripture. The form of the communication, as Steudel suggests, may be accounted for by the supposition that the author's first intention was to write a treatise as a guide to the brethren in their perplexity, and the more so that his want of personal acquaintance with his readers made this appear the more seemly course; but, in the management of his argument, the natural warmth of his disposition led him into the epistolary mode. We are committed to the opinion that Hebrews is an Epistle, for if we are right in regarding what is now spoken of as Peter's *Second* Epistle as having been addressed to the Jewish section of the Church at Rome, then Hebrews was Peter's *First* Epistle to these brethren there. And, if the piece was not begun as an Epistle, though it fell into the epistolary style, this is quite sufficient to account for the omission of the name.

(β) Peter was known to his readers by reputation at least, and they were well aware who it was that was writing to them. Might not Peter have omitted his name for prudential reasons? When this Epistle was written, the Jews, and especially those of them who had adopted the Christian faith, were in bad odour at Rome. If it had become known that an Epistle had come to the brethren there, or to a section of them, from so well known a follower of Christ as Peter, this would certainly have not only intensified the hostility against them, but might have made the apostle's position a dangerous one in the event of his fulfilling his promise to visit them. There was evident need for secrecy. It is easy to conceive how, in these circumstances, what was well known at the time to a section of the Church gradually dropped out of sight. In the troubles of the period even the destination of the Epistle might be lost to view.

(γ) The Epistle was intended only for a section of the Church at Rome, not for the whole of it. This may be the reason, and it seems a sufficient reason, why the Epistle wants, not only the author's name, but also any hint as to its destination. Peter, in his modesty, may have meant his production to be regarded as very much of the nature of a private document, for the immediate satisfaction of those who had applied to him for counsel.

## II

# MELCHIZEDEK—HIS PRIESTHOOD AND PERSONALITY

### PART FIRST

THERE is no subject within the whole compass of biblical literature which interpreters have felt to be more fascinating than than of Melchizedek, and there is no other which has given rise to more discussion—learned and otherwise. The books and treatises which it has called forth would, if gathered together, form a very extensive library. And almost every day the mass of literature on the question is being added to. There is at present an inquiry on foot, inspired by the hope of being able to discover, in the vague realms of archæology, a race of priest-kings to which those prosecuting the inquiry believe Melchizedek belonged. Of all the vain dreams which this subject has begotten, we have no hesitation in saying this is the vainest. Those who pay any attention to the way in which the question is dealt with in Scripture can have no difficulty in predicting that such an inquiry is a wild goose chase, and can do nothing but bring ridicule upon those who are pursuing it. Archæology has its uses, but not in this case.

Some curious results have emerged from the dis-

## Melchizedek's Priesthood and Personality 35

cussion of this subject. Some have been driven to the conclusion that no satisfactory explanation is possible, and that any one who meddles with the matter is guilty of "rushing in where angels fear to tread." In the opinion of such persons, any one who is bold enough to undertake the exposition of the matter must be afflicted with some form of insanity. Some think they are warranted to treat the question as fair game for ridicule and mirth, and are always ready with the well-known story of Dr. Chalmers and his unwelcome visitor. Others think we are guilty of serious irreverence if we essay to apply the ordinary rules of grammar and interpretation in this case. All references which Scripture makes to Melchizedek must be understood in a kind of slip-shod way. They are too peculiar to be brought within the limits of sound exegesis. You must deal with this subject as you deal with no other in the sacred volume. As a rule, however, such persons have no hesitation in delivering their opinions with the utmost confidence. You would expect them, in the circumstances, to avoid all dogmatic utterances, and to merely hint at what they suppose may *possibly* be the meaning of the sacred writer who deals with the matter. This is by no means the manner which they adopt. They decide the meaning of every phrase with the most perfect assurance that their dicta cannot be disputed. A fair example of this class of interpreters is the present Dean of Canterbury —Dr. Farrar. This popular writer and preacher, in the *Sunday Magazine* for 1886, thus expresses himself: "Scripture has undergone strange perversions at the hands of its interpreters,—perversions which fill the minds of simple truth seekers, sometimes with sadness, sometimes with indignation." This is the first sentence of the worthy Dean's paper, and is intended to prepare the way for the condemnation of all who differ from him on this question. He takes the view, now generally prevalent, that Melchizedek was a type of Christ. Farther on he indulges in this *ex cáthedra* strain: "Apollos,—or whoever was the author of this Epistle,—writing to show that the Aaronic priesthood was annulled, chose another priest —Melchizedek—the first man who in the Bible is called 'a priest'—as the type of Christ's priesthood. He seizes upon a partial analogy between him and Jesus in saying that he was 'without father, without mother, without descent, having neither beginning of days nor end of life.' The phrase is a very simple and very common figure of speech, found in all languages. Beyond all question, it means nothing more than that neither his father, nor his mother, nor his pedigree, nor his birth, nor his death are anywhere recorded. They are facts practically non-existent, because we know nothing about them; and, therefore, as he stands on the page of Genesis, Melchizedek furnishes, even in this respect, a fit type of the eternal Christ. 'Oh! but it is childish,' say the commentators, 'to think that the sacred writer means no more than this.' It is, I reply, not merely childish, but gratuitously absurd, to interpret his conceptions by any other law than those of the language which he used, and the terms in which he wrote. It was the fashion of the Alexandrian School to which he belonged to see Allegories, and to attach mystical secondary meanings to the slightest details, and even (as in this passage) to the accidental silence of Scripture." Our view traverses that of Dr. Farrar at every point, but we confine ourselves here to one remark only. His assumption that the author of "Hebrews" was of the Alexandrian School is totally void of any support from the Epistle. It is simply the creation of his own imagination, or rather of the imagination of those whose opinions he submissively accepts. It is an inference drawn from a certain interpretation *put upon* the exposition of the sacred writer in Heb. vii. In that chapter, as we hope to be able triumphantly to show, there is not a jot or tittle of the kind of reasoning usually ascribed to the Alexandrian School.

The views which have been held on the subject under discussion range themselves in two groups. Some have held that Melchizedek was a mere man. Dr. Farrar, whose words we have just quoted, is an example of this class. Others have regarded him as a supernatural being. Within both groups there is a considerable variety of opinion. We do not, however, intend to enter into any examination of the modifications of opinion within these two groups. We limit ourselves to the general question whether Melchizedek was a mere man or a supernatural being. This is really the essence of the controversy. If our inquiry leads us to the conclusion that he was, and, of course, in that case is still, a supernatural being, as we expect to be able conclusively to show, it will be an easy task to determine who this supernatural being must be.

As we have already hinted, it is now almost universally held that Melchizedek was a mere man, and a remarkable representative of pure religion in the midst of a heathen and idolatrous race. So deeply rooted is this opinion, that we were recently told by a Professor of Theology in one of our Colleges, that no one now ever thinks of calling it in question. All modern writers treat the question as completely settled. We regret deeply this state of matters, for we believe this view is quite inconsistent with the statements and arguments of Scripture. It is deeply dishonouring to the word of God. It presents the writer of the Epistle to the Hebrews more in the light of a dealer in rabbinical whimsicalities than as an inspired exponent of divine truth. It really involves the consignment to discredit of a very precious portion of the word of God. This casuistical exposition, if it be such, interpolated in the middle of a noble Epistle, is the fly which spoils the whole apothecary's ointment. If it be really a reproduction of what was in the mind of the writer when he wrote that part of the Epistle which relates to this subject, then the whole production must be rejected as that of an unprincipled sophist. The so-called reasoning which it presents is an open insult to our intelligence. And this is really, for the present writer at least, a most serious matter. If there were no other way of explaining what our author says of Melchizedek than that which the commonly received view presents, he sees no alternative before him but to reject the Epistle as uncanonical. He is fully persuaded, however, that this view totally misapprehends the meaning of the sacred writer, and puts a violent and perfectly unnatural construction upon expressions which are in themselves luminously plain and easily understood. After a very prolonged and careful study of the subject, he is thoroughly convinced that the natural and unsophisticated construction of all that the Bible says on the subject is quite sufficient to vindicate the Epistle to the Hebrews from all suspicion of sophistry, and to demonstrate that it contains nothing which is inconsistent with truth and soberness.

To show the bewildering effects produced upon some acute minds by the acceptance of the commonly received view, we shall here make two quotations. They are from the pens of two authors of very different schools of thought. The first is from Matthew Arnold's *Literature and Dogma*, 2nd ed. p. 269 : "The 7th chapter of Hebrews, again, is one tissue of clever, learned trifling, such as we might have from the Bishop of Gloucester, all based on the false assumption that 'Thou art a priest for ever after the order of Melchizedek' was really said to Jesus, whereas it was not." There is quite a sufficiency of dogmatism here ; but let that pass. If we accept the view of Melchizedek now generally entertained, with all the violence to language which it implies, it is impossible to deny that the 7th chapter of Hebrews is "a tissue of clever, learned trifling." No other words could so accurately describe the state of the case. Our other quotation is from "Papers on Hebrews," by the Rev. Prof. A. B. Bruce, D.D., in the *Expositor* for 1889, p. 97 : "He (the author of Hebrews) gets at the ideal by laying stress on the *silences* as well as the *utterances* of the narrative in Genesis. Whatever we may think of his method of reasoning, there can be no doubt of the fact that he does so reason, and the fact must be frankly recognised, if we are to get at his real thought. He finds, for example, that no mention is made of the parentage or genealogy of Melchizedek, and he regards that as significant." All who know Dr. Bruce admire the fearless courage with which he declares what he believes to be the truth. He honestly thinks that the commonly received view of the personality of Melchizedek (which he accepts) is that of the author of Hebrews, and he declares accordingly. He believes that the truth is able to take care of itself. On the other hand, we are satisfied that he, and all those whose view he represents, misunderstand the author with whom they deal, and, of course, unintentionally betray the truth. He errs in thinking that the warrant for calling Melchizedek parentless is taken from the passage in Genesis. The author finds authority for this and all those other expressions which have occasioned so much difficulty in connection with his exposition from Ps. cx., as we shall show by and by. Dr. Bruce evidently thinks that his author argues in a very questionable manner. Can he, cherishing such an opinion, now whole-heartedly accept the Epistle as inspired and canonical? But what can a plain unlettered Christian think, after reading such words as those of Dr. Bruce? He will surely say, if that is a correct representation of what the author of the Epistle to the Hebrews says, I must now discard that Epistle altogether as no longer entitled by me to be called the word of God.

It is evident that in a discussion of this kind very much depends upon the method of procedure. If our method be faulty, in all probability the result will be unsatisfactory. Three courses are open for our choice. (1) We may begin, as Dr. Farrar and Dr. Bruce do, with what is recorded in, or rather not recorded in, Genesis, and, putting our own construction on what we do not find there, make all that is elsewhere said bend to that construction. The unwisdom of this method is demonstrated by the results attained. Besides, it is manifestly unscientific, and opposed to the principles of sound interpretation.

It is taking an obscure passage—one admittedly invested with mystery—and using that to explain passages which have no mystery in them whatever. (2) We may begin with what we find in Hebrews, note what is said about Melchizedek there, and then draw our inferences. This is certainly a much more scientific method than that to which we have just referred. This method has been adopted by some more or less formally, and with results more or less satisfactory. It has, however, its disadvantages. It is like attempting to unravel a tangled clew of thread without concerning ourselves about finding the end. (3) We may, in thought, place ourselves in the position in which our author was placed when he began to deal with this subject, and may patiently follow him as he develops, out of Genesis, and particularly out of Ps. cx., all that is found in the 7th chapter of Hebrews. This course should commend itself to our readers. It will put us on a pedestal from which we shall be able to survey the whole field, and will enable us to perceive the weakness of the arguments advanced in support of the commonly received view. It will place us side by side with our author, and enable us to see how he proceeds.

But before entering upon the pursuit of this method, which we shall adopt, we must attempt to clear away some of the obstructive matter which has gathered around the subject in the course of ages. (1) It has been very persistently affirmed that the author of Hebrews asserts that *every high priest is taken from among men.* From this the inference is drawn, that Melchizedek must have been a mere man. The affirmation is supposed to be warranted by the words of ch. v. : " For every high priest, taken from among men, is ordained for men in things pertaining to God," etc. The Revised Version reads, " Being taken from among men." The original word is λαμ-βανόμενος. It may be translated as is done by the Revisers, or as by the Authorised Version, or by the words " who is taken from among men." This last is undoubtedly the meaning. The author of Hebrews does *not* affirm that *in every case* a high priest is taken from among men. He simply asserts that, when this is done, he " is ordained for men," etc. Surely no one is so blind as to be incapable of seeing that this is a very different thing from saying that " every high priest is taken from among men." It is not true, as matter of fact, that every high priest is taken from among men. Aaron and his sons were so taken, and set apart by divine warrant and authority to their sacred office. Their function was to offer gifts and sacrifices for the sins of the people. *Christ, when appointed to the priestly office, was not taken from among men*, but was the eternal Son of God. He became man, but it is quite incorrect to say that He was taken from among men. The affirmation which we are combating is a very dangerous one. If we accept it, we shall have to deny the divine and eternal high priesthood of Christ. It is clear, therefore, that no argument to prove that Melchizedek was a mere man can be founded upon this passage. It comes upon us as a galvanic shock that any interpreter, and especially any evangelical interpreter, should for a moment dream of putting forward such an argument.

And yet this is only an illustration of the strange expedients which have been adopted to explain away the natural meaning of the statements which the author of Hebrews makes regarding the eternal priesthood. In the 4th verse of this same 5th chapter it is said, " No man taketh this order to himself but he that is called of God, as was Aaron." We must bear in mind that all that is said in this Epistle was intended for Jews. And we must try and put ourselves in their place if we are fully to understand its teaching. The quotation just made applies only within the bounds of the Mosaic economy. When high priests have been appointed in connection with other religions, they have not received the divine sanction, and have not been "called of God," as Aaron was. If they have not appointed themselves, they have been appointed by other men. As Aaron was appointed to the high-priestly office by God, so was Christ—" So Christ also (ver. 5) glorified not Himself to be made a high priest, but He that spake unto Him, 'Thou art My Son, this day have I begotten Thee.' As He saith also in another place, 'Thou art a priest for ever after the order of Melchizedek.' " In addition to all that we have here said, we may add that the affirmation that every high priest *is taken* from among men is not only theologically, but also grammatically, impossible. $Λαμβανόμενος$ is not the principal verb in the sentence, and does not convey a definite proposition.

(2) It is affirmed that the subject of Melchizedek is invested with impenetrable and insuperable difficulty. And the inference is drawn, that it is hopeless to look for anything like a satisfactory elucidation of the matter. This affirmation is supposed to be warranted by the words in Heb. v. 11: " Of whom we have many things to say, and hard of interpretation, seeing ye are

dull of hearing. For when by reason of the time ye ought to be teachers, ye have need again that some one teach you the rudiments of the first principles of the oracles of God," etc. Now, assuming, for the sake of argument, that these words refer to Melchizedek, for the reference is by no means indisputable, is it not clear on the very surface of the passage that the difficulty is, by our author, ascribed, not to the subject itself, but to the mental condition of the Jewish converts? If this is not so, then words have no meaning. The reason assigned for the difficulty is nothing in the nature of the case, but *dulness of hearing*, that is, spiritual obtuseness on the part of the author's readers. Those, therefore, who bring forward this passage as a proof of the mystery connected with the subject of Melchizedek, unwittingly confess that they deserve the unflattering character here ascribed to those to whom *Hebrews* was addressed. Because the subject, for the reason assigned, presented a difficulty to certain Jews, it does not follow that every one must experience the same difficulty. It is evident that the writer himself felt no such difficulty. We have no right, certainly, to complain, if men speak disparagingly of their own powers of understanding, but we protest against their using such liberties with us. The Christians of our day are far in advance of those converted Jews to whom *Hebrews* was addressed, and they are unfairly treated when this difference is overlooked. If the Jews in our author's day found a difficulty in understanding what was said about Melchizedek, that is no warrant for saying that all Christians in our day must do the same. If the minds of the Christian Jews addressed in this Epistle had been in a proper state, they would have had no difficulty in following every word which our author uses. Is it not evident that, by interpreting the passage now before us, as indicating an inveterate and impenetrable mystery in the subject of Melchizedek, we are writing ourselves down as in the same unhealthy spiritual state as those converted Jews whom our author so soundly rates? According to the argument of the sacred writer, we should have no difficulty in understanding his words, if our minds are in anything like a spiritually vigorous condition.

But has our author not kept something back? Has he not dealt with his readers as our Lord did with His disciples when He said: " I have many things to say unto you, but ye cannot bear them now"? And has not this reticence occasioned the difficulty which the subject now possesses? There is no evidence whatever that anything has been kept back.

It would be a strange procedure to blame people for dulness of understanding, and at the same time keep back what was necessary to make the matter plain. If our author has kept back anything necessary to the understanding of the subject, then he, and not his readers, is to be blamed for any difficulty that is felt. He has simply befooled them—and us. He has excited our curiosity, and then, tantalisingly, has failed to satisfy it. But we cannot believe this. And, if the mystery does not arise from what is omitted, where is the warrant for suspicions about omissions? What our author has given us he must have considered sufficient for explanation. If he has kept back all that it would be difficult for us to understand, and that can be the only conceivable reason for omissions (if he has made any), there should be no difficulty at all about what he has given us. But the truth is, such obstructions to interpretation as we are trying to remove—for they do not deserve the name of arguments—are far more difficult to deal with than sound reasonings. There is sufficient haziness about them to make them perplex and confuse the reader. We cannot believe that our author has left out anything from his exposition that was essential to its completeness. Every point is fully, carefully, and clearly argued. If readers do not understand our author, the fault is certainly not his.

We have been arguing as if the reference in the passage under consideration were to Melchizedek, and not to Christ. We must now consider whether we have been right in so arguing. Does not the relative, *of whom* (οὗ), refer to Christ, and not to Melchizedek? This is primarily a question of grammar, but it has also a most important bearing upon the matter of exposition. The difficulty, both as to the grammar and the meaning, arises from the fact that the name of *Melchizedek* had to be mentioned at the end of the 10th verse. But the whole discussion in the preceding part of the chapter is about *Christ*. The immediate object of the sacred writer is to establish the truth that Christ was made a high priest by divine appointment. Reference is made to Ps. cx. to confirm this point. And as in that reference the word *Melchizedek* occurs immediately before the relative, *of whom*, it is argued that this must be the antecedent. This is to misapply the grammatical rule, that the relative refers to its nearest antecedent. Circumstances may obscure the application of this rule, and such circumstances occur here. Commentators have allowed their minds to become confused by the

## His Priesthood and Personality 47

writer's reference to what is contained in Ps. cx. They have overlooked the fact that the application of the grammatical rule is obscured by the mention of Melchizedek's name, and have allowed themselves to be persuaded into the belief that our author, at this point in his Epistle, leaves the subject which he has been discussing, and turns aside to that of Melchizedek. They confound the real with the seeming antecedent. If the 10th verse, which contains the reference to Ps. cx., be included in brackets, for the sake of argument, the construction will become perfectly clear. Then we read, taking with us the 8th and 9th along with the 10th verse for the sake of connexion, "Though He was a Son, yet He learned obedience by the things which He suffered; and having been made perfect, became to all them that obey Him the author of eternal salvation (named of God a high priest after the order of Melchizedek), *of whom* we have many things to say, and hard of interpretation, seeing ye are dull of hearing." Thus read, the antecedent to *of whom* (οὖ) is 'the author of eternal salvation." Unless, indeed, we conclude that our author here, on purpose, mixes up Melchizedek and Christ in the relative *of whom* (οὖ). The former idea is preferable. Either one or other view, however, is in harmony with what follows: "For when, by reason of the time, ye ought to be teachers, ye have need again," etc. To interpret the words in question otherwise than of Christ, or, at all events, so as to exclude Christ, is to overlook the drift of the writer's reasoning, and to assume that, at this point, he goes off at a tangent. It is easy to understand why the converted Jews should be blamed for their spiritual backwardness in matters connected with Christ, but it is difficult to understand why they should be censured for their inability to comprehend statements about Melchizedek, and, especially so, if he was a mere man. What, in that case, could Melchizedek have to do with their spiritual advancement? The author of the Epistle to the Hebrews was angry with them because they were backward in understanding about Christ.

There is in the 7th verse of this same chapter a construction exactly like that which we have been trying to make plain. Here also the application of the grammatical rule is obscured by the quotation of the oracle in Ps. cx.: "Who in the days of His flesh, having offered up prayers and supplications with strong crying and tears unto Him that was able to save Him," etc. Here the nearest antecedent to *who*, if the passage is carelessly read, seems to be *Melchizedek* at the end of the 6th verse, which contains the quotation from Ps. cx. All interpreters now admit that, notwithstanding the closest proximity of the relative to *Melchizedek*, the real antecedent is not *Melchizedek*, but *Christ*. This is an exact grammatical parallel to the case we have dwelt upon so long. In both cases the application of the grammatical rule is obscured precisely in the same way. This should be strongly corroborative of the view we have taken of ver. 11. But the matter is so clear that we hardly think any of our readers will seriously dispute our position.

We admit that the subject of Melchizedek is surrounded with some difficulty. The matter is not so simple that it can be taken in at a glance. After the keen controversy which it has excited, it would be absurd to assert the contrary. But, as we have already pointed out, the difficulty arises more from human infirmity or perversity than from the statements of the sacred writer. The subject is not insuperably difficult, as we hope to be able to show, if we allow our minds patiently to follow the course of thought pursued by our author. His whole exposition of the matter in question arises beautifully and naturally out of the materials with which he has to work. He has his text, or rather his two texts, and he keeps closely by them. No preacher in the present day could expound his texts more faithfully, or more logically. His exposition is a masterpiece of compact reasoning.

Before passing from introductory matter, there is one other point to which we must call attention. One of the main objects of the Epistle to the Hebrews is to establish, in a way to satisfy the Jewish converts of the time, the eternal priesthood of Christ. In no other part of the word of God does this important subject receive formal discussion. And in no other part of the New Testament is the word *priest* applied to our Lord. His atonement and work are referred to elsewhere, but it is only here that He receives His official title of *priest*. This indicates the vital importance of what is here advanced. The preciousness of this part of Scripture becomes further apparent when we consider that all our hopes of eternal life hang upon the doctrine of Christ's priesthood. And it was surely to be expected that the Spirit of God would take care to see that this doctrine was established upon a firm and immovable foundation. It would appear that the Jewish converts of the time had very loose and imperfect notions on the subject. They did not clearly understand that the sacrifices and priests under the Law pointed to the one sacrifice of Christ and His priestly functions. They had been brought up under the Mosaic economy, which had been appointed by God, and which they believed to be perfect and unalterable—a system never to pass away or be disannulled. It is easy to understand how, in these circumstances, they found it difficult altogether to abandon views which they and their fathers had cherished for long generations, and how, after they became Christians, they should hanker after their earlier sentiments. It was to be expected that they would require careful and convincing arguments to overcome the effects of their early training and habits. Human reasonings, apart from the plain declarations of the word of God, or some direct communication from heaven such as was received when the Law was inaugurated, could not be accepted as possessed of any weight. What divine authority had sanctioned, divine authority alone could set aside. Apart from the miracles which were wrought in attestation of Christian truth, no extraordinary intimation of the mind of heaven was necessary, provided explicit statements could be found in their own Scriptures bearing on the subject. It would not be enough for any one to claim that he was inspired of God to make known to them a change in the divine methods. At least, this would not be so satisfactory as the production of explicit evidence from their own Scriptures on the point. And that evidence must be put before them in a well-reasoned form. Our author being a Jew himself, and well aware of the feelings of his kinsmen regarding the Law and the Levitical priesthood, and being an intelligent follower of Christ and fully satisfied in his own mind regarding all the doctrines of the Christian faith, he was also well aware of the steps which he required to take in order to establish young

Jewish converts in this cardinal doctrine of Christianity. To any one who has felt the difficulty of shaking off early religious opinions and of contending against commonly received beliefs, the discussion of this subject of Christ's eternal priesthood must be possessed of intense interest.

In this doctrine, then, our author seeks to establish the minds of his readers. These were haunted with the fear that they were doing wrong in ignoring the priests under the Law. In seeking to remove this haunting fear from their minds, our author adopts a course similar to that which Paul adopts in the Epistle to the Galatians when seeking to establish the doctrine of *justification by faith*. He finds a priesthood spoken of in Genesis long prior to the institution of the Levitical priesthood, and, in the Book of Psalms, written long after the institution of the Levitical priesthood, an oracle constituting Christ a priest according to the order mentioned in Genesis. The whole Mosaic system, including the Levitical priesthood, was a mere temporary arrangement devised by God for the training of His people. When they came out of Egypt, they were quite unfit to appreciate the divine method of salvation, and it was found to be necessary to embed the truth in a setting of rites and ceremonies, out of deference to their spiritual and intellectual weakness. In the course of time this system of rites and ceremonies became an intolerable burden, as the nation became more and more enlightened and passed out of its childhood state. The oracle in Ps. cx., given long after the institution of the Levitical priesthood, must be regarded as setting that priesthood aside, and as re-establishing that mentioned in the Book of Genesis. And this is what our author seeks to prove in Heb. vii. He carefully elaborates the comparison which is made in that Psalm between Melchizedek and Christ.

---

## PART SECOND

We can hardly appreciate the argument in Heb. vii. without first trying to realise for ourselves the position in which its author was placed when he commenced the discussion there presented, and without keeping distinctly before our minds the materials with which he had to work. There was, first of all, the narrative in Gen. xiv. It will hardly be questioned that, if we had had no other information than is found there, we would have unhesitatingly concluded that Melchizedek was simply an extremely pious, God-fearing man who lived in the midst of an ungodly race, and held forth the banner of truth in the worship of the one living and true God. But our method of viewing that narrative has been materially affected by what we find recorded in other parts of Scripture. Our eyes have been thereby opened to perceive that there is an air of mystery about it which a cursory reading of it does not at first disclose. Melchizedek appears on the scene suddenly, and then disappears as suddenly. We are told that he was *a* priest of the Most High God, or rather, *the*[1] priest of the Most High God. He blesses Abraham, and that patriarch pays tithes to him. The mystery about this personage deepens when we realise that not one word is given

---

[1] The article used in Heb. vii. 1 before Μελχισεδέκ applies not only to that word, but also to βασιλεύς and ἱερεύς.

us indicating further intercourse between him and the patriarch. If he were an earthly monarch and a mere human priest, such as the narrative seems *primâ facie* to indicate, how is it that we do not read that Abraham took up his abode within his dominions? And how does it come about that the kings who attacked Lot did not make an inroad on his kingdom? Such a peaceful sovereign must have presented strong temptations to plunder for a company of heathen marauders. But, confining our thoughts to the Jews, the respect and deference which Abraham showed to Melchizedek must have induced the Jews to look upon him with no small measure of reverence and awe. They must have said to themselves, He could be no ordinary man who thus assumed superiority over the friend of God, and from whom the great head of the Hebrew race accepted a blessing.

This mystery continued for many generations unrelieved by any ray of light from heaven. During that period, no doubt, the imagination of God's ancient people often turned towards the personality of Melchizedek in the endeavour to fathom its mystery. Some would form one conjecture regarding him, some another. Then came the oracle in Ps. cx. But the author of that psalm does not entirely remove the mystery left around the subject by the narrative in Genesis. He, however, gives us a little more light in a particular direction. He brings more vividly before our minds Melchizedek's priestly office. He does not tell us definitely who Melchizedek was, but he presses upon our notice the fact that his priesthood is eternal. "Thou art a priest for ever after the order of Melchizedek." This is a distinct addition made to our knowledge. It enables us to think of him more definitely than we could have done had not the information in Genesis been supplemented in this way. It is true that it is not the immediate object of the sacred writer in this oracle to satisfy our curiosity about Melchizedek. We get this additional information regarding him in an indirect way. The immediate purpose of the Spirit is to disclose and declare the eternal priesthood of Christ, but this is done in such a way as to make it plain that what is true of the priesthood of Christ is also true of that of Melchizedek. If Melchizedek is not a priest for ever, neither is Christ. The order of Melchizedek's priesthood is distinct from, and superior to, that of Aaron; the one is eternal, the other is merely temporal. The duration which is ascribed to the priesthood of Christ is by the terms of the oracle ascribed also to that of Melchizedek. Both belong to the same order, and any peculiarity which belongs to the one belongs also to the other. Special attention is now in Ps. cx., for the first time, called to this order, but it has existed from all eternity.

The perfect correspondence between the priesthood of Melchizedek and that of Christ, as declared in this psalm, has been very generally overlooked by commentators. The oracle has been read as if the priesthood of Melchizedek were inferior to that of Christ, as the type is inferior to the Archetype. For this idea there is not a shadow of a shade of warrant. Not a single word is used to convey the idea that Melchizedek was inferior to Christ. The two stand on a footing of perfect equality. We are not now concerning ourselves about any consequences to which the recognition of this fact may lead. We are following the strictly scientific method of first getting at

## His Priesthood and Personality  55

the facts before making any attempt at drawing conclusions. We cannot allow the progress of our inquiry to be interrupted by any objections that may arise as to how there can be said to be, or seem to be said to be, two eternal priests. We must take words in their plain and natural meaning. We are not warranted in setting aside a plain and natural sense till we find that by following it we involve ourselves in absurdity. We are quite aware of the objection which presents itself to some minds at this point, but we shall cross the bridge when it is necessary, not before. Meanwhile, we pursue the even tenor of our way. One thing at a time is a very good rule in most cases.

We do not here enter upon any inquiry as to the date of Ps. cx. The object we have in view does not require us to do so. Suffice it to remember that it was in existence when the author of the Epistle to the Hebrews undertook his task. It had probably been in existence for many generations, and its contents pretty well known by the Jewish people. Its statements being well known, through being often sung, would help to prepare the people's minds for the use which our author makes of one of its verses. The authorship of this psalm is, by our Lord, ascribed to David, when He says to the Pharisees (Matt. xxii. 41–45), "While the Pharisees were gathered together, Jesus asked them a question, saying, What think ye of Christ? whose son is He? They say unto Him, The son of David. He saith unto them, How then doth David in spirit call Him Lord, saying, The Lord said unto My Lord, Sit Thou on My right hand, till I make Thine enemies Thy footstool? If David then call Him Lord, how is He his son?" An important help in connection with our present discussion is furnished by this passage which we have quoted from the Gospel narrative. It satisfies us that Ps. cx. is Messianic, and that, Matthew Arnold notwithstanding, the words in ver. 4 were really said to Christ. These words, as we have already seen, declare that Melchizedek is a priest for ever, and that Christ is a priest of the same order. This point cannot be too strongly emphasised. If the oracle had merely said that Christ was a priest for ever, this would not have so fully met the necessities of the case. It would not have shown the inferiority of Abraham to Melchizedek, and the inferiority of the Aaronic priesthood to that of Melchizedek, and, consequently, to that of Christ. The object was to prepare for the setting aside of the Aaronic priesthood as well as to establish the eternal priesthood of Christ. The peculiar mental attitude of the Jews seems to have rendered it necessary to put the oracle in this way.

All the materials, then, with which our author had to work were taken from these two sources—the narrative in Genesis and Ps. cx. He introduces into his discussion in Heb. vii. not one thought which is not perfectly warranted by his authorities. His whole argument there clearly and logically arises out of the narrative in Genesis, along with the words of the oracle in Ps. cx., especially the latter. And he founds no argument on silence. He finds clear and positive evidence in his authorities for everything he says. This may sound strange to some ears, but it is a fact notwithstanding. And it is to us a most surprising circumstance that this peculiarity has been so imperfectly realised throughout this controversy. It has been either entirely overlooked, or only in part apprehended. The usual way of looking at the matter is to credit the author of *Hebrews* with originating, by a fertile imagination, certain ideas out of the narrative in Genesis. These ideas are *negative*, as they are supposed to originate in that narrative, but by a kind of intellectual legerdemain they become *positive*, and are dealt with in the same way as documentary evidence. How this transformation is accomplished we, at least, are utterly unable to conceive. Suppose counsel in a court of law were to endeavour to manipulate his evidence, or rather want of evidence, in this way, who can doubt that the judge would make short work with him? We may safely say, no counsel would be so foolish as to make the attempt. And how writers can reconcile themselves to the thought that men, under the guidance of the Spirit, could reason in this way, baffles our comprehension. If the argument for the eternal priesthood of Christ were by our author built up in this way, it would rest on a foundation of sand. If a Jew were to understand that the oracle in Ps. cx. meant that the priesthood of Melchizedek was *sui generis*, having no predecessor and no successor, and that, therefore, Christ's priesthood is for ever, we could hardly expect him to look upon such an argument with much respect. And, instead of such an argument tending to confirm him in the Christian faith, it would have a precisely opposite effect. It could appear to him in no other light than as a piece of barefaced sophistry.

The connexion between Heb. vi. and vii. is very close. This connexion is indicated by the use of the conjunction *for* (γάρ). And as our author reproduces in a particular order the words of the oracle in Ps. cx. which he quotes at the close of ch. vi., it will conduce to clearness if, before going farther, we give a translation of the last paragraph of that chapter, together with two or three words at the beginning of ch. vii.: "For men assuredly swear by the greater, and with them an oath for confirmation puts an end to all dispute. In view of this, God, wishing to show more abundantly to the heirs of the promise the immutability of His purpose, confirmed it with an oath, so that by two immutable things in which it is impossible for God to lie, we might have a powerful encouragement—we who have fled for refuge—to lay hold of the hope set before us, which we have as an anchor of the soul, a sure and steadfast one, and which has entered into that within the veil, whither as a forerunner for our sakes has entered Jesus, who, according to the order of Melchizedek, has become a high priest for ever (εἰς τὸν αἰῶνα). For this Melchizedek," etc.

Our object in so carefully translating this paragraph is twofold. (1) We wish to show the close connexion between chs. vi. and vii. (2) We wish to call attention to the particular manner in which our author quotes the oracle in Ps. cx. The order of the words as they stand in Ps. cx. is, "Thou art a priest for ever after (or according to) the order of Melchizedek." Here the order is, "Who according to the order of Melchizedek has become a high priest for ever." The words are evidently arranged in this order for the purpose of leaving it without dispute that the phrase, "According to the order of Melchizedek," means the same thing as the other phrase, "A priest (or a high priest) for ever." This careful collocation of words, which our author has adopted, is not indicated in either the Authorised or the Revised Version. In the psalm, the clause, "According to the order of Melchizedek," stands last. Our author in the instance now under consideration puts it first, though in all other cases he follows the arrangement of the psalm. Now, what can his object be in making the quotation in this way on this occasion? For, that he has an object, no intelligent student of Scripture can doubt. The words, as they stand in the psalm, possess a certain measure of obscurity. They make it plain that Christ is a priest for ever, but they do not make it so plain that Melchizedek is a priest for ever. By the manner in which our author arranges the words, as quoted at the close of ch. vi., this obscurity is entirely removed. They now bring out the idea that Christ is a priest for ever, because He belongs to the order of Melchizedek. That is, in this instance the fact is made prominent that Melchizedek is a priest for ever. The priesthood of Melchizedek and the priesthood of Christ are both qualified by the words *for ever.* All this is perhaps plain enough; but, because of the importance of the subject, let us try and illustrate the point further by a supposed example. Eleazar was, according to the order of Aaron, a mortal priest. If we met with a statement of this kind, what conclusion would we be entitled to draw from it? Most assuredly, that the one was a mortal priest as much as the other, no less, and no more so. The inference is irresistible. No sane man would dream of calling it in question. It is true, we know that Aaron was mortal, but we would have been entitled to draw the same conclusion if we had known nothing about him beyond what is stated in the illustration used. Our author, in arranging his words in the order to which we have called attention, lays an immovable foundation for everything in ch. vii., which distinguishes Melchizedek from mere men, and which has caused so much perplexity to commentators. If the expression *for ever* is, in the case of Christ, a true and proper attribute of eternity, it is so also in that of Melchizedek. The way in which our author quotes the words of the oracle in Ps. cx. renders it necessary that we should so understand it. He forbids us, as it were, to limit its meaning when applied to Melchizedek, while at the same time taking it in its full sense when applied to Christ. We would only observe, before leaving this point, that our author uses the term *high priest*, instead of simply *priest*, because he has been speaking of Christ passing within the veil in allusion to the high priest going into the holy of holies on the great day of atonement.

Our author having thus removed all ambiguity from the oracle in Ps. cx. by his manner of quoting it, now gathers up into one long sentence (ch. vii. 1–3) all that he finds in his two texts, at least all that is necessary to his purpose. "For this Melchizedek, king of Salem, priest of the Most High God, who met Abraham returning from the slaughter of the kings and blessed him, to whom also Abraham divided a tenth part of all—being first, by interpretation, King of Righteousness, and then also King of Salem, which is King of Peace—a person without father, without mother, without genealogy, having (*since he has*) neither beginning of days nor end of life, but resembling (*since he resembles*) the Son of God, abideth a priest continually." Here the statement, *This Melchizedek abideth a priest continually*—εἰς τὸ διηνεκές, first claims our attention. This is the truth which our author wishes now to bring into prominence. And it was for this purpose that he quoted the words of the oracle in Ps. xc. in the order in which we find them at the close of ch. vi. The words now before us are an assertion founded on Ps. cx., that the priesthood of Melchizedek is, like that of Christ, eternal. The expression εἰς τὸ διηνεκές is synonymous with the phrase εἰς τὸν αἰῶνα. They both mean *for ever*. If anyone is inclined to think that the priesthood of Melchizedek is inferior to that of Christ, he should now be fully disabused of his false impression. Not only the fact that the words under consideration are, on the face of them, an inference grounded on the words of the psalm, and formally introduced by the word *for*—γάρ—but also the expression employed, should be sufficient completely to banish from any one's mind all idea of Melchizedek's inferiority to Christ.

The phrase εἰς τὸ διηνεκές is evidently used instead of εἰς τὸν αἰῶνα simply for the sake of elegant variety. Its precise meaning must be determined by the context in which it occurs. It is used other three times in this Epistle: ch. x. 1, " For the law, having a shadow of good things to come, not the very image of the things, they can never with the same sacrifices, year by year, which they offer continually,—εἰς τὸ διηνεκές," etc. In the same chapter, ver. 12, " But He, when He had offered one sacrifice for sins for ever,—εἰς τὸ διηνεκές—sat down," etc. In ver. 14 of the same chapter we read, " For, by one offering He hath perfected for ever —εἰς τὸ διηνεκές—them that are sanctified." After these examples, it will be difficult to maintain that the words εἰς τὸ διηνεκές are used by our author in any sense that means less than *for ever*. We would merely remark further here: Our author's word is *abideth*, not *abode*. Melchizedek is a priest now, and will continue a priest *for ever*. Nothing is said about Melchizedek bringing forth bread and wine, for the obvious reason that this was in no way necessary to his argument. It is to be observed, also, that every particular mentioned here is used in the subsequent part of the chapter to establish our author's position. This is a fact which deserves to be noticed with particular emphasis. The full force of this fact has not hitherto been felt, because the peculiar construction of the sentence has not been apprehended. If that construction be carefully followed, as we have endeavoured to indicate it in our translation, every thing at once becomes luminous and plain.

The key to the meaning of every thing in the sentence lies in the participles *having* (ἔχων) and *resembling* (ἀφωμοιωμένος). Any one who carefully reads over the sentence will, on coming to the word *having*, feel that there is a peculiar turn given to the construction at this point, and which arrests the mind. So much force is there in this remark that many, whose minds are imbued with the ordinary view, cannot read the sentence correctly, but must treat it as if it ran thus: "Without beginning of days or end of life." Even some of those who otherwise take what we regard as the correct view of the personality of Melchizedek fall into the same manner. It may be said, indeed, that it is no uncommon thing to find people misquoting passages of Scripture. It is to be observed, however, that there is something special in this case. The misquotation is always made in the same way. This surely points to a common misapprehension of our author's meaning. And had our author intended to convey the sense which the ordinary view presents, he would naturally have employed the phraseology of his misquoters.

It is not enough to say that the word *having* introduces an agreeable variety into the construction. If that is all our author's object in thus varying his phraseology, the variety is not only not agreeable, but is the very reverse. The pleasant flow of thought is rudely interrupted. The effect is like that produced upon a horse when it is suddenly reined in.

We have very much pleasure in referring, in this connection, to the words of Bishop Westcott. He denies that it is possible to regard the remarkable variation of our author's language, which occurs at this point, as due to mere rhetorical ornament.[1] When we came across this declaration, we confess that our heart began to beat somewhat quickly. We imagined, for the moment, that this acute and accomplished scholar had stumbled upon a discovery which we had hitherto thought was all our own. This discovery we made while a student well-nigh forty years ago. As we continue, however, to read what Dr. Westcott has to say, we soon learned that we had not been forestalled. His statement, which caused us so much temporary excitement, came to nothing. He has failed to perceive the reason for the change of construction. On the very point of making what we claim to be a most important discovery on this absorbing subject, this learned and acute bishop failed to see the whole length.

As we have already said, on the supposition that Melchizedek was a mere man, this construction arrests the easy and natural flow of thought and language, and altogether looks like an uncouth stumbling-block

[1] *The Epistle to the Hebrews: The Greek Text, with Notes and Essays*, 1889, p. 173.

in the reader's way. Admitting, for argument's sake, the correctness of the common or typical view of the personality of Melchizedek, with how much more pleasure would we have read: " Without father, without mother, without genealogy, without beginning of days or end of life"! There must be some other explanation of this change in our author's phraseology than that which refers it to variety of style. Perhaps some of our readers have already been inclined to call in question our quotation of our author's words, and to say to themselves, Does not the author of Hebrews actually write *without beginning of days or end of life*?

We venture to say that no satisfactory explanation of this admittedly striking construction is to be found, unless we regard *having* and *resembling* as causal participles, assigning the reason why Melchizedek is described as " without father, without mother, without genealogy." We have an example of a similar construction in the well-known passage 1 Tim. iv. 8, " Godliness is profitable for all things, having (since it has) promise of the life that now is, and of that which is to come." But we hardly required to quote an example of such a construction. Every grammarian knows that examples of such a construction are abundant. Our only surprise is that scholars have not long ago discovered that the two participles referred to are causal. To our mind the thing is self-evident.

The importance of this interpretation of the two participles in Heb. vii. 3 will, we trust, be clearly seen by our readers. We have, however, had some difficulty in convincing some of our friends on the point, and in getting them to admit that, even if they are interpreted as we say they should be, this contributes anything to the elucidation of the subject.

We wish to point out with all the emphasis at our command that, when we so take these participles, we are at once directed to our author's authority for all those statements which he makes concerning Melchizedek, and which interpreters have found to be so difficult to account for. We then perceive that he does not evolve those statements out of the silence of Scripture. We discover warrant in Ps. cx. for all his expressions which are deemed peculiar. It is here that we find the *positive* evidence appealed to in the words, "Of whom it is witnessed that he liveth." We discover that this is, in fact, *documentary* evidence such as would be admitted to be irrefragable in a court of law. It is just such evidence as Jews were bound to admit to be satisfactory.

Moreover, this interpretation of the participles in question gives a force and compactness to our author's words which they cannot in any other way be shown to possess. We are sanguine, therefore, that this part, at least, of our contribution to the literature of Melchizedek will meet with the approval, not only of the general reader, but also of scholars. Observe the clearness and consistency of all our author's statements about Melchizedek when we read the participles in question as causal. Melchizedek resembles Christ in being without father, without mother, without genealogy, because both are without beginning of days or end of life. They are coeternal. We have nothing to do with objections in the meantime. All that we have to do at this point is to note facts. The removal of objections will come in due time. The Alpha privative in the words ἀπάτωρ, ἀμήτωρ, ἀγενεαλόγητος indicates what is absolutely true. We must not let our minds here be confused with the ideas of God being the Father of Christ as respects His divine nature, and Mary His mother as respects His human nature. If we do so for a moment, we are at once confronted with the fact that, as regards His human nature, our Lord had a genealogy. Christ is without father, without mother, without genealogy, as the eternal, coeternal Son of the Father. We must not allow our minds to think of Christ as the Son of the Father in the same sense as a mortal man is his father's son. Christ is not the Son of the Father in that sense. Melchizedek, whoever he was (for we are not now discussing his personality), was in all the respects we have mentioned perfectly like Christ. We are not to think of Christ as having become a priest at His incarnation, or even from the time when the oracle in Ps. cx. was pronounced, for that was merely the declaration of a fact already existing. Christ was a priest from all eternity. Equally so Melchizedek is declared to be such a priest. We cannot evade this conclusion without twisting words out of their natural meaning. This is the one point of resemblance upon which our author dwells, for it is the only one on which he is warranted by Ps. cx. to dwell. He exhibits this point in various lights. It is because interpreters have not clearly apprehended this fact that they have fallen into so much confusion. When our author's exposition is fully understood, it turns out to be a beautiful, logical discourse, founded on his two texts, particularly the oracle in Ps. cx. If Melchizedek was really a mere man, as the typical view represents him to have been, we cannot acquit our author of dishonesty in saying that he was without father, without mother, and without genealogy, for, as man, he must have had all three.

If he had no posterity, he must, at least, have had ancestors. It is not honest to argue that he had no father, etc., because these are not recorded in Scripture, or in genealogical tables.

The writer of these pages claims the credit of having discovered the true character of the participles in Heb. vii. 3, which totally changes the whole complexion of the Melchizedek controversy. He hopes his sense of the importance of his discovery will be accepted as his excuse for making this claim. He had never in the whole course of his reading met with the faintest hint that the participles should be so taken, when the idea occurred to him. Some may be inclined to call in question the validity of this claim when they read the following sentence in the published Lectures of the late William Lindsay, D.D., Professor in the United Presbyterian Divinity Hall, vol. i. p. 323: "*Having* is certainly causal, but not in respect of the other members, all being on a level, and all causal of *abideth*." He means by *members*, undoubtedly, members of the long sentence beginning with ver. 1 and ending with ver. 3. We shall explain immediately how this sentence comes to be printed in the Lectures at all, but meanwhile we have to remark—(1) Dr. Lindsay's words, though they at first sight appear to be a statement of our view, really mean something very different. He admits, it is true, the causal nature of *having*, but he immediately explains away that admission. It is, he says, no more causal than any other clause in the sentence. We really find it exceedingly difficult to make sense out of the Professor's words. But they seem to amount to this, that every clause in a sentence is causal of the main proposition. This may be true, but it is not the idea which grammarians attach to the phraseology when they speak of a causal participle. But (2) instead of Dr. Lindsay having forestalled us in the discovery that the participles in question are *causal* (he mentions only the one—*having*,—but the use of the particle δέ indicates that the other—*resembling*—must be put in the same category), we can prove that the word was suggested to him by ourselves. We are sorry that he got hold of the word without being able to grasp what the word implies. As one of his students, it was our good fortune to listen to most of his lectures on Hebrews. As he approached the subject of Melchizedek, and seemed inclined to accept the erroneous typical view, as we even then regarded it, we ventured, privately, to ask him whether taking *having* and, consequently, *resembling* as causal participles did not put a new complexion on the words of the author of Hebrews, and throw a desirable light on the whole controversy about Melchizedek. The Professor replied to our view in the class-room, but without mentioning our name, in the spirit of the sentence which we have quoted, and with considerable elaboration of argument. We felt the reply to be exceedingly unsatisfactory, in fact we failed to follow him, but had not at the time the courage to say so, and allowed the matter to drop. Our readers will notice that the words of the sentence bear on their face that they are meant as a reply to some one. This is clear from the word *certainly*. Moreover, the sentence has a look somewhat foreign to the context in which it occurs. These circumstances satisfy us that they are intended as a reply to our view. When the Lectures were published after the Professor's death under the editorship of his friend the late Rev. George

Brooks, M.A., minister of the United Presbyterian Church, Johnstone, near Paisley, we were very eager to find out how the matter as to the sentence in question stood. To make assurance doubly sure, and to discover whether the Professor had really been before us, even in applying the word *causal* to the participles in question, or either of them, we wrote to his learned editor, asking if the sentence referred to was in the body of the Lectures as originally prepared, or was an interlineation, or if there was any evidence that it had been written after the Lectures had been composed. We were very promptly favoured with the following reply:—" Dear Sir,—I have to report that the sentence you quote was certainly added after the Lectures were composed, and is hurriedly written on the blank page.—Yours truly, George Brooks."

## PART THIRD

It is not essential to our object to enter upon a complete exposition of Heb. vii. We are not writing a commentary. Our author's object was to bring into prominent view every point in which Melchizedek's priesthood was superior to that of Aaron. Our object, on the other hand, is simply, in the first instance at least, to establish the eternal character of Melchizedek's priesthood in the strict and proper sense of the word. We must therefore pass over much in this chapter which the commentator is bound to notice. Thus we pass over the argument founded on the fact that Abraham paid tithes to Melchizedek, as that argument is present in the paragraph vv. 4–7 inclusive. We would here merely repeat the remark, which we have already emphasised, that there is not in this paragraph which we pass over, any more than in any other part of the chapter, the slightest hint that either Melchizedek or his priesthood was in the least respect inferior to Christ or His priesthood. Abraham was inferior to Melchizedek, but Melchizedek is never mentioned as inferior to Christ. The assertion of the contrary is one of the most glaring defects of the commonly received view.

We come to the words in ver. 8: "And here men that die receive tithes, but there he receiveth them of whom it is witnessed (or testified) that he liveth." There is here, first, a contrast as to time; the period referred to in Genesis is contrasted with the period at which our author was writing. But there is, secondly, this far more important contrast—that between Melchizedek and the Levitical priests. There is this essential difference between the latter and the former—they die, but he lives; they are mortal, but he is immortal. Earnest attempts have been made to elude the force of our author's statement here, but in vain. No amount of sophistry can explain away the natural meaning of his words. It will not do to say that the meaning is, that Melchizedek is living, because we have no account of his death. We are not in the custom of reckoning those of whose death we have no account as still living. Above all, we never think of contrasting such persons with mortal men, as if they belonged to a better and nobler race of beings. Where, on such an exposition, is there any semblance of an argument for the eternal priesthood of Christ? If those whom our author was seeking to establish in this doctrine understood him in this sense, would they not have treated his words with contempt? And would they not have been justified in so treating them? Do men who use arguments of this kind never think how ridiculous they must appear in the eyes of infidels. Nor will it do to read the words as if the reference were to Christ and not to Melchizedek. Such an interpretation is completely excluded by the reference to the historical fact that Abraham paid tithes to the person here indicated. There is more plausibility about the argument founded upon what our Lord said to the Sadducees about the resurrection, "Now, He is not the God of the dead, but of the living." Some would argue that our author's meaning is that Melchizedek lives, simply in the sense that Abraham, Isaac, and Jacob now live with God. That is, as they now live in glory, so does Melchizedek. If that were the idea, there could be no propriety in contrasting Melchizedek with mortal men; for Abraham, Isaac, and Jacob were mortal men, just as certainly as any one else of the human race. And they are not the only sons of Adam who are now inheriting eternal life. Was our author such a fool as to lead an argument of this kind? No, there is no way of explaining the words in question but that which assigns to them their plain and natural meaning. Whoever we make out Melchizedek to be, our author's assertion is, that he is living now; at least, he was living when this Epistle was written. And, if he was living when our author wrote, we need have no difficulty in accepting the words before us in the absolute sense, and saying that *he is living now*. Thousands of years elapsed between the days of Abraham, to whom Melchizedek appeared, and the time when *Hebrews* was written, and at that time Melchizedek was living.

But our author appeals to some *witness* in favour of his position that Melchizedek is now living. "Of whom (or concerning whom) it is witnessed, that he liveth." This is surely something very different from the assertion that we have no evidence of his death. There are a good many people mentioned, both in Scripture and elsewhere, of whose death we have no account. But we do not, for that reason, say that it is witnessed concerning them that they are still living. It is one thing to say that we have no evidence for or against any point, and quite another thing to say that we have positive evidence for it. To our mind, it is quite inconceivable how any one can confound the two things. In a court of law the difference which they imply is all-important. Let us suppose a case. A question arises as to whether any particular person is alive. The succession to, and administration of, an estate depends upon the settlement of this question. Evidence is led to the effect that the person was living as an adult at a certain date, say one hundred and fifty years ago. No trace of him can be found subsequent to that date. Here, then, is a mixture of positive and negative evidence. But the negative evidence becomes absolutely positive when we remember that no one in modern times has been known to live, say one hundred and seventy years, for we have been supposing that the person was an adult at the time for which positive evidence of his existence was produced. Would a court of law have any difficulty in deciding that the man is now dead? There could be no question of the fact after such a lapse of time. If a legal heir came forward, there would be no difficulty in his securing possession of the estate. According to the reasoning of some in connection with the question of Melchizedek, the lawful heir, in this case, could not enter upon possession, because there is no positive evidence of the former owner's death. Would any lawyer in the land have ingenuity enough to formulate out of the facts of the case this legal position, *Of whom it is witnessed that he liveth*? We have only to look at the matter in this plain, common-sense way to see the absurdity of the argument *e silentio*.

If Melchizedek was a mere man, we did not require to be told that he died, for all men die; but if he was not a mere man, though he assumed mortal flesh for a temporary purpose, it was necessary to make us aware of this by telling us that he did not die—that, in fact, he is living now. An attempt has been made to escape from the natural meaning of our author's words by saying that there may be a reference to some statement in some book now lost. We do not see how this can in the slightest degree affect the question. If Melchizedek was a mere man, he is now as certainly dead as any other man who ever lived. It cannot, therefore, be maintained of him that he is living. But here, as again and again throughout the whole of this discussion, we are confronted with questions as to the divine authority of this Epistle, and as to the foundation on which the eternal priesthood of Christ rests. We cannot conceive of any testimony furnished by any book, lost or existing, which could warrant our author in saying that a mortal man, supposing Melchizedek to have been such, is now living. Can we suppose that the Holy Spirit has rested the great fundamental doctrine of the eternal priesthood of Christ on such a basis? What must unbelieving Jews of the present day think of such an argument?

Who, then, is the *witness* to whom our author refers? Those who have followed our argument up to this point hardly require to be told. Our author's witness is the Spirit of God, speaking by the mouth of the author of Ps. cx. We would say *of David*, but the higher critics have such strange ways of dealing with such matters that we are afraid to speak our mind. We do not wish to come into collision with such champions. If Melchizedek is a priest for ever, then he must be living, for we do not say a person is a *priest* after he is dead. When we read the words *having* and *resembling* in Heb. vii. 3 as causal participles, we see clearly that our author's witness is the writer of Ps. cx. It is to our mind a convincing proof that, down in the depths of the Christian heart, there lies the conviction, that the absurd arguments which the learned men who have written on the subject of Melchizedek have used do not express the mind of the Spirit, that this Epistle has not been long ago treated as forming no part of God's revealed will.

We pass on to the paragraph vv. 15–17: "And the matter is still more abundantly evident, if after the likeness of Melchizedek there ariseth another priest who hath been made, not according to the law of a carnal commandment, but according to the power of an endless life, for the testimony (or witness) is, Thou art a priest for ever according to the order of Melchizedek." Here some of our author's expressions may seem a little unusual, but the meaning is clear enough. There is, on the surface of his words, an evident anxiety to avoid, if possible, the danger of being misunderstood. The variety of statement which he employs reminds us of St. Paul's words in Ephesians, where he states the manner of a sinner's salvation in four different ways: "By grace are ye saved through faith; and that not of yourselves: it is the gift of God: not of works, lest any man should boast." As in this quotation from Ephesians, the different clauses in the paragraph with which we are now dealing explain one another. Our author begins by speaking of Christ as a priest according to the order of Melchizedek. Then he explains this language, first, *negatively*, and then *positively*. (1) To be "a priest after the likeness of Melchizedek" does not mean, to be a priest "after the law of a carnal commandment," that is, such an arrangement as is suited to the case of mortal men. These are not permitted to remain in the priestly office by reason of death. There must in this case be an arrangement for a succession of priests. The law of the Levitical priesthood made men priests who die, and, therefore, required others to succeed them. Christ did not become a priest under such a law. (2) To be a priest "after the likeness (or order, or style) of Melchizedek" means, to be a priest "according to the power of an endless life," that is, by virtue of an arrangement which subsists for ever and ever. The priesthood of Melchizedek belongs to immortals. Melchizedek has an endless life; and, as Christ is a priest of the same order, He too has an endless life and priesthood. There is much meaning in our author's word *power*. It conveys the idea that Christ is a priest according to another arrangement than that which made the sons of Aaron priests. That law was, by its very nature, unsuited to Him; and His eternal divinity exalted Him far above it. The law of the Levitical priesthood was a mere temporary arrangement, and belonged to a mere temporary priesthood. Christ has been a priest from all eternity, and is "the Lamb that hath been slain from the foundation of the world." Here again, as throughout the whole discussion of His priestly office, Christ is viewed, not as a mere man, but as the eternal and immortal Son of God. As the eternal Son of God He never died, and could not die. As the sacrifice for the sins of the world, His humanity, which He had assumed for the purpose, died; though after a time restored to life again: as the sacrificing priest, He did not, and could not, die.

The words, "after the likeness of Melchizedek," deserve further notice. Some have affirmed that our author teaches that Melchizedek was made like Christ, but not that Christ was made like Melchizedek. Such a remark can arise only from the grossest carelessness. It is apparently sanctioned by the ambiguous translation of ἀφωμοιωμένος in ver. 3. This word, strictly interpreted, means simply *resembling*, as we have rendered it in our translation of the paragraph in which it occurs. It has been erroneously taken by the Revisers of 1611, and their successors of 1881, as intended to convey the idea that Melchizedek was divinely appointed to be a type of Christ. The words now under consideration completely refute this idea. They warrant us in saying that, if the words in ver. 3 give any one ground for asserting that Melchizedek was divinely appointed to be a type of Christ, then the phrase, "after the likeness of Melchizedek," would equally give ground for saying that Christ was divinely appointed to be a type of Melchizedek. The phrase κατὰ τὴν ὁμοιότητα (after the likeness, or, according to the likeness) means precisely the same thing as ἀφωμοιωμένος (resembling, or being made like). Both phrases arise out of the oracle in Ps. cx. By the terms of that oracle, Melchizedek is declared to be like Christ, and Christ is declared to be like Melchizedek. The resemblance is mutual and complete.

There is yet another expression to be noted with emphasis before we leave this paragraph. We refer to the words, " The testimony (or witness) is, Thou art a priest for ever according to the order of Melchizedek." These words make it plain that the *witness* referred to in ver. 8, and upon which we have commented at some length, is the oracle of the Spirit by the mouth of the writer of Ps. cx. The word for " the testimony (or witness) is," in this paragraph, is μαρτυρεῖται; that used in ver. 8 is μαρτυρούμενος. It is impossible to escape from the force of such an argument. The positive documentary evidence for the statements which our author makes about Melchizedek, when these statements seem to be remarkable, is Ps. cx. Why cannot the indisputable fact be admitted? We do not need to go to archæology for any explanation of our author's words.

We have now seen that the resemblance between Melchizedek and Christ, as brought out in this discussion, is mutual and complete. We have not found one item of proof to justify us in saying that the one is in any respect inferior to the other, or to encourage any one to think that the one is a type of the other. We can claim that the method of inquiry which we have pursued has been scientific throughout.

What are we now to make of the result of our somewhat lengthened inquiry? We have come to the question, Who is this who is represented as bearing so complete a resemblance to Christ, feature for feature? The idea of certain of the early Christians, as Epiphanius tells us, was, that he was some great power, superior to Christ, and who is now exalted to places not to be named. This theory seems to have been founded, so far, on the scientific method, but has been exploded long ago. Hierax and others, also in early Christian times, thought Melchizedek was the Holy Ghost, because it is said that "the Spirit maketh intercession for us with groanings that cannot be uttered." The Holy Spirit is never, however, called a *priest*. A priest is one who offers sacrifices, but it is never affirmed in Scripture that the Spirit sacrifices. There remains only the other possible opinion, that Melchizedek was Christ Himself. This is the opinion to which we have been compelled to give our assent. This opinion is mentioned by Epiphanius as having been held by some in very early Christian times. It has been assented to in different periods of the Church's history by some of the most scholarly and acute minds which Christianity has known. We believe this view would have commanded universal acceptance long ago if the argument had been presented in anything like a complete form. To complete this argument two missing links have hitherto been awanting. These we have endeavoured to supply. (1) The careful and rigid exhibition of the comparison between Melchizedek and Christ, as that is presented in Ps. cx., and (2) the proof that ἔχων (having) and ἀφωμοιωμένος (resembling) are causal participles. By so regarding these participles we obtain positive warrant for the words ἀπάτωρ, ἀμήτωρ, ἀγενεαλόγητος, and all the other expressions which have proved such stumbling-blocks to interpreters hitherto. These all arise, with perfect logical justness, out of the oracle in Ps. cx.

## His Priesthood and Personality

Our argument here must of necessity assume an inferential form. Our object is different from that of the writer of *Hebrews*. His great aim was to establish the eternal priesthood of Christ. He does so by proving that it is precisely of the same character as that of Melchizedek. He did not require to go farther. On the other hand, *our* object is to determine the personality of Melchizedek. Our author wished the Jews to cease hankering after the Levitical priesthood, as an old and effete institution which had served its day. He finds a solid foundation for his argument in the eternal priesthood of Melchizedek. He did not require, for the purposes of his argument, to say who Melchizedek was. Our object takes us beyond the point at which he stops. In this pursuit we do not act inconsistently with the spirit of his argument. Nor are we seeking to be wise beyond what is written. We believe that our inference is thoroughly well founded. In this part of our discussion we are but following the course which our author has pointed out. He has spread out before us the materials essential for the decision of the point. He has led us by the hand up to the sublime height of Christ's eternal priesthood. There he has left us, flushed with the curiosity which his words have irresistibly begotten within us, to pursue to its logical termination the pathway along which he has so far led us.

(1) Our first argument for the identification of Melchizedek with Christ is founded on the peculiar form of words used in Heb. vii. 1: Οὗτος γὰρ ὁ Μελχισεδέκ, βασιλεὺς Σαλήμ, ἱερεὺς τοῦ Θεοῦ τοῦ ὑψίστου. Our position here is, that the article ὁ must be taken as belonging, not only to Μελχισεδέκ,

but also to βασιλεύς and ἱερεύς. That is, Melchizedek is here declared to be κατ' ἐξοχήν, *the* priest of the Most High God. Unless we take the article in this way, no difference is made to appear between Melchizedek and Abraham, who, as the head of his family, was *a* priest of the Most High God. And one of the main objects of our author is to show Melchizedek's superiority over the old patriarch. There is a grammatical parallel in 1 Pet. v. 8, 'Ο ἀντίδικος ὑμῶν, διάβολος, which our Revisers render, "Your adversary, the devil."

(2) Our second argument is drawn from the fact that an eternal priesthood is ascribed to both. There cannot be two eternal priests, according to all the teaching of the New Testament. One of the duties of a priest is to mediate between God and man, but the Scripture tells us, "There is one Mediator between God and men, the man Christ Jesus." No created being, how exalted soever, can be co-mediator with Him. We have no doubt that our author was fully aware of the identity of Melchizedek with Christ, but apparently there was some reason for his not saying so.

(3) Our third argument is drawn from the fact, which we have noted several times, that our author is at pains to show that the resemblance between Melchizedek and Christ is complete. He has taken care not to write one word calculated to convey the idea that Christ is in anyway superior to Melchizedek. This is very significant. Let us endeavour to bring out a little more distinctly the force of this fact. We find descriptions given of two apparently different persons. These descriptions perfectly correspond, letter for letter. We happen to be perfectly

acquainted with the one person. As we compare the descriptions, and perceive that it is impossible to detect any feature of dissimilarity, we say to ourselves, Why, these descriptions belong to one person, and not to two! They are accounts of my friend by two different individuals! We must either admit that Melchizedek is Christ, or confess that there must be two eternal priests.

(4) Our fourth argument is drawn from the fact that our author is at pains to translate the names assigned to Melchizedek, rendering them *King of Righteousness* and *King of Peace*. We can see no other object which he could have in view in doing so, than to provide his readers with an argument in favour of the identity of the two persons. The translation of the words does not affect his main argument in the slightest degree. It would not be a sufficient reply to our reasoning here to say that names mentioned in Scripture are sometimes very significant. We are speaking of the translation of significant names. The writer who translates a name must always have an object in so doing. It must either be for the instruction of those who do not understand the language to which the name belongs, and do not in consequence see its appropriateness or significance; or to throw some new light upon what is being said. Now, this Epistle was addressed to Jews, who may be supposed to have had some acquaintance with the Hebrew language to which the words *Melchizedek* and *Salem* belong. Why, then, should our author have burdened a long sentence with the translation of Hebrew names, if he did not wish to give his readers and us hints intended to carry us farther than the purpose of his own argument required him to take

us? The most natural explanation of this translating of the names in question is to be found in the fact that these names are given to our Lord in the Old Testament. Jesus is called by Jeremiah the Lord our Righteousness, and Isaiah speaks of Him as a King who should reign in righteousness. By the same prophet He is also called the Prince of Peace. These names of Christ, taken in connection with our author's translations, *King of Righteousness* and *King of Peace*, are surely very significant. We are really unable to see any reason why our author translated the names referred to, except to lead his readers to identify Melchizedek with Christ, without doing this himself in express terms. We think, as we shall see immediately, that there was a reason for his not proceeding to the actual step of identification. But there is another point, not without its significance, to be noted before we leave this argument. Why does our author use the words *first* and *afterwards*? "Being first by interpretation," etc. Is this not to indicate the order of experience in the sinner's heart when Christ and His truth are received? There is, first, repentance, or the craving for righteousness, and then the peace which passeth all understanding. "The work of righteousness shall be peace; and the effect of righteousness, quietness and confidence for ever." Surely there is some designed coincidence in all this.

The fact that Christ appeared on several occasions in different characters in Old Testament times is a very powerful confirmation of those arguments which we have just advanced. All sound theologians admit that Christ did so appear. For example, He appeared to Abraham as the Judge of all the Earth, in connection with the destruction of Sodom. He seemed to rejoice in the habitable parts of the earth, and to have His delights with the sons of men. Why should men stumble at the idea that Melchizedek was an Old Testament Christophany? If he appeared in other characters, why might He not have appeared as *the* priest of the Most High God. Besides, what satisfactory explanation can be given of the conduct of Abraham towards Melchizedek, unless we believe that he regarded Him as a divine person? He could hardly have treated a mere man as he treated Him. Can we believe that he who had the promises, and in whom all the families of the earth were to be blessed, could bestow such honour as the narrative in Genesis shows Melchizedek to have received, upon a mere Canaanitish prince, however worthy he might have been, belonging as he did to an accursed race? This would be tantamount to showing such honour to the whole race represented by their prince. Can we believe that the solemn interview which the patriarch had with Melchizedek was with a mere man?

It has been made evident by the whole course of this discussion, that the oracle in Ps. cx. gives us fuller information concerning Melchizedek than that supplied by the narrative contained in Genesis. We could never have thought of Melchizedek as an eternal priest, if the oracle had not so described him. This oracle also gives us a fuller revelation concerning Christ than has hitherto been received. This is quite in harmony with God's method of revelation. He has given His Church a fuller and fuller revelation of His will as time advanced. But, if we are right in identifying Melchizedek with Christ, the question naturally arises, Why was the oracle in Ps. cx. put in the form in which we find it? Why not simply declare that Christ is a priest for ever? There are several answers which may be suggested to such a question. First of all, we must allow God to reveal His will in His own way. Then there is the evident advantage in favour of the form in which we find the oracle, that it maintains the law of continuity. What is said in Genesis becomes a stepping-stone to what is declared in the psalm. Besides, the oracle in Ps. cx. connects the eternal priesthood of Christ with a priest to whom Abraham showed the greatest reverence, and from whom he accepted a blessing, thus admitting Melchizedek to be greater than himself; for without all contradiction the inferior is blessed by the superior. And by paying tithes to Melchizedek, Abraham, as the father of the Hebrew race, was practically, for the Levitical priests, paying tithes to the same person. That is, when Abraham paid tithes to Melchizedek, the Levites practically paid tithes. All this showed the superiority of Melchizedek's priesthood over the Levitical, and prepared the way for the setting aside of the latter. Then, further, I think we may safely assume that there was some reason in the mental attitude of the Jews that prevented them from being able to accept a plain didactical revelation regarding the eternal priesthood of Christ. Some device had to be fallen upon to induce them to accept this truth. We can see how this was effected through the instrumentality of the oracle in Ps. cx. The Holy Spirit, seeing beforehand the way in which they would become prejudiced in favour of the Levitical priesthood, fell upon the expedient of uttering this oracle. By putting it in a psalm it was made certain that the people would become well acquainted with it. Then, the Jews clung tenaciously to what their Scriptures contained. All classes, as we see from the Gospel narratives, held themselves bound to abide by all that could be proved out of the Scriptures. The wisdom of putting the oracle in the form in which we find it is then, we think, manifest.

But is this form of the oracle not of doubtful character ? Or rather, is our whole view of it not somewhat suspicious ? Can we point to anything parallel to this way of speaking of a person, as if he were not one, but two. We follow something like the same course every day. We receive a photograph of some individual. We make ourselves acquainted with the features there pictured to us. Then, we meet with an individual whom we have never seen before. For the time being the photograph and the individual represent two persons. But we proceed to compare the features in the photograph with those of the individual standing before us. We find that the features of the two exactly correspond, and we come to the conclusion that we have before our view only one and the same person. We do this all the more quickly and all the more confidently if, in the case supposed, the features are very prominently marked. Melchizedek is, as it were, a photograph of Christ.

The same method of revelation adopted in the oracle of Ps. cx., is adopted in Rev. i. 12 : " And I turned to see the voice which spake with me. And, having turned I saw seven golden candlesticks ; and, in the midst of the candlesticks, one like unto the Son of Man, clothed with a garment down to the foot, and girt about at the breasts with a golden girdle. And his head and his hair were white as white wool, white as snow ; and his eyes were as a flame of fire ; and his feet like unto burnished brass, as if it had been refined in a furnace; and his voice as the voice of many waters. And he had in his right hand seven stars; and out of his mouth proceeded a sharp, two-edged sword; and his countenance was as the sun shineth in his strength." When this vision was vouchsafed to John, he was in much the same position as the reader of Ps. cx. before our author expounded the meaning of the oracle. He had in his mind two pictures—Christ, and some one like Him. He was able to see that the two pictures were one, only when Christ Himself so taught him.

If the line of argument which we have pursued throughout the whole of the discussion be in harmony with the mind of our author, there can be no force in the objection taken to our view long ago by Epiphanius, and made so much of by subsequent writers, that a man cannot be said to be like himself. This likening of Christ to Melchizedek, and of Melchizedek to Christ, arose out of the necessities of the case. It was the result of the form in which the oracle was given. Nor can any weight be attached to the objection that the word *order* makes it necessary that we should hold Melchizedek and Christ to be two different persons. We are not sure that the word may not be employed to describe a priesthood, even though only one individual belongs to it. But this objection is really the former one in another form. The word *order* seems to be used because the oracle, for the sake of revelation, had to be worded as if there were two eternal priests, and not merely one.

We hope we have succeeded in removing from this Epistle the reproach which certain commentators have brought upon it. And we wish to say that our study of this subject has wonderfully deepened our admiration of the intellectual subtlety and theological grasp of our author. We no longer believe that Paul is the only theologian of the New Testament, if, as we believe, he was not the writer of this Epistle.

Many books, as we have said, have been written upon the subject which we have endeavoured to discuss. There is one which we have made many unsuccessful efforts to secure, Borgesii, *Historia Critica Melchizedeci*, Berne, 1706. This book is referred to by many writers, but whether all who refer to it have seen it is another question. Dr. Kitto refers to it in his *Biblical Cyclopædia* under the name *Borger*. The late Dr. W. L. Alexander, who edited the *Cyclopædia*, slavishly copies the title of this book as given by Kitto, thus showing that he had never seen it. We have written to the author of the article on Melchizedek in the *Schaff-Hertzog Cyclopædia* (who mentions the book at the close of his article), asking him if he could give us any information where the book could be seen, or bought. Several months have elapsed, but we have received no reply to our most courteous note. The only inference we can draw is that, like Dr. Alexander, he has never seen the work, but thought fit to append its title to his article to give it the appearance of erudition. If anyone can favour us with a sight of the book, we will esteem it an especial kindness.

*Note.*—Since writing the above we have had the opportunity of examining this much-referred-to volume. We came upon a copy in the Royal Library at Berlin in the summer of 1897. The book has deeply disappointed us. It professes to discuss all the questions which have been agitated in connection with Melchizedek. The author's management of these questions is by no means such as to entitle him to be quoted as the great authority on the subject. He takes the view which *is* now popular, and against which we have written. The only reason we can see why his work is so frequently referred to in articles on the subject of which *it* treats is to be found in its pretentious title. It is somewhat suspicious that while it is so much referred to by those who write about Melchizedek, it is very seldom quoted. Indeed, its statements are hardly worth quoting. It would be easy to mention works in which the views which the author holds are both better expressed and better defended. It is time that theologians ceased to refer with deference to a book which has really so little to recommend it. But till we had seen it we had the uneasy feeling that it might contain something which we ought not to overlook.

# III

# CHRIST'S OBJECT IN PREACHING TO THE SPIRITS IN PRISON

## An Exegetical Study

"Ὅτι καὶ Χριστὸς ἅπαξ περὶ ἁμαρτιῶν ἔπαθε, δίκαιος ὑπὲρ ἀδίκων, ἵνα ἡμᾶς προσαγάγῃ τῷ Θεῷ, θανατωθεὶς μὲν σαρκὶ ζωοποιηθεὶς δὲ πνεύματι, ἐν ᾧ καὶ τοῖς ἐν φυλακῇ πνεύμασι πορευθεὶς ἐκήρυξεν, ἀπειθήσασί ποτε, ὅτε ἀπεξεδέχετο ἡ τοῦ Θεοῦ μακροθυμία ἐν ἡμέραις Νῶε, κατασκευαζομένης κιβωτοῦ, εἰς ἣν ὀλίγοι, τοῦτ' ἔστιν ὀκτὼ ψυχαί, διεσώθησαν δι' ὕδατος· ὃ καὶ ὑμᾶς ἀντίτυπον νῦν σώζει.

"Because Christ also suffered for sins once, the righteous for the unrighteous, that He might bring us to God—put to death because of the flesh, but restored to life because of the spirit. Wherefore (*literally*, In which) He even went and preached to the spirits in prison, who were at the time disobedient, when the long-suffering of God was continuing to wait in the days of Noah, while the ark was a preparing, into which few, that is, eight souls, were brought safely through water. And this also is now saving you an antitype."
—1 Pet. iii. 18-21*a*.

EXPOSITORS generally have pronounced the passage before us to be one of great difficulty, and the various and conflicting interpretations which have been given of it bear out this testimony. It would be a very hard task to have to mention two commentators of any eminence who explain it exactly in the same way, or who are agreed as to what it teaches. If all that has been written upon it were brought together, it would make a library of considerable extent, and form a mass of literature as perplexing as has ever been produced on any subject.

There are some who profess to think lightly of its alleged difficulties. But these are not generally men whose expositions are the most satisfactory to others, how much soever they may seem to be so to themselves. The meaning can be determined only by the most careful exegesis. Mere dash, or assumption of confidence, will not give satisfaction to the thinking reader. We believe, however, that the day is not far distant when the alleged difficulties will be no longer felt, and when it will be matter of astonishment that these should ever have occasioned perplexity. Let the pious learning of the Church of the present day take the matter up in thorough earnest, and if it follow faithfully the principles of sound exegesis we shall soon see this result.

Many learned men have attempted an exposition. Why is it still left in obscurity? For this simple reason: its would-be interpreters have persisted in following a theory of construction which leads to results, not only perplexing, but in sharp contrast with the plainest teaching of Scripture elsewhere. The construction which they accept is by no means necessary, and the results which it leads to should be enough to prove that it is erroneous. Yet no other has hitherto been thought of. Some one in early times gave the passage a false twist, and all subsequent writers have followed his lead with ludicrous persistency. This is all the more to be wondered at, since another mode of construction yields a sense at once simple, natural, and scholarly, and in line with the great fundamental doctrines of revelation. We propose to show that this construction brings out the true meaning of the apostle.

There are some who look upon any attempt to expound such a passage as that now before us as presumptuous and unprofitable. Against such an idea we most earnestly protest. It is a reflection upon the wisdom of God, and is dishonouring to His word. It is a practical rejection of a portion of divine truth. Whatever God has been pleased to write for us in the Scriptures, it is our duty diligently, earnestly, and lovingly to study, and with the conviction that it is calculated to promote our edification. To treat any portion of Scripture as those to whom we refer would have us treat that now before us, is to strike at the root of the great truth, that " all Scripture is profitable." Some pious minds can indeed rest contented without giving themselves any concern about difficult passages, but with others it is different. They must try and get at the root of the matter, and must form some opinion regarding their teaching. The history of the past abundantly demonstrates this. It is therefore the sacred duty of every one who thinks he can explain any passage of the Bible which has hitherto been regarded as encompassed with insuperable difficulty to bring forward his light for the benefit of the Church. He who shall have the privilege to settle the interpretation of the passage before us will have done a work worth living for. What a benefit would such a service be to the cause of truth!

So wild and contradictory have been the opinions which some have built upon this portion of God's word that many have become settled in the conviction that no satisfactory solution of the difficulties which it presents can ever be found. Can we regard such a conviction as sound or intelligent? Does it not rather savour of scepticism? At least, this is not a view of the matter with which we ourselves have any sympathy. When expositors fail to make any portion of the word of God clear, the fault is to be assumed as resting with them, not with the Bible.

In some minds there seems to be a vague impression that the apostle has here fallen into inextricable confusion. The popular idea regarding the ignorance of the apostles lends some colouring to this impression. If they were the ignorant men which some take them to have been, what more natural than that they should have sometimes fallen into confusion? But with this popular idea regarding the apostles we are at complete variance. Their writings prove them to have been the very reverse of ignorant. And the more one studies these writings the deeper becomes the conviction of the accuracy and appropriateness of the words which they employ. There was no confusion of thought in their minds when they wrote. And this is not to be wondered at when we remember that they wrote under divine inspiration. In his Second Epistle our apostle speaks of " the unstable and unlearned " in a way which shows that *he*, at least, did not regard himself as belonging to this class. It is very significant that the writers of Scripture never call themselves ignorant. Had they so spoken, they would have reflected upon God, for He taught them; and they would most effectually have robbed themselves of all confidence, and justly so. When Peter and John were brought before the Sanhedrim for preaching the gospel, the members of that august assembly were astonished at the wisdom of their answers, though they were, in their estimation, *unlearned and ignorant men*, that is, not men absolutely such, but men who had not been trained under recognised Jewish rabbis. The conduct of the apostles on that occasion proves that they were anything but ignorant in the ordinary sense of the word. No one who is intelligently acquainted with his Bible can hold by the opinion that Peter fell into hopeless confusion in the passage before us.

In that part of the Epistle in which the words which we propose to examine occur, the apostle is exhorting his readers to patience in the endurance of any sufferings which they might be called upon to bear. They seem to have been subjected to serious trials and persecutions. To induce them to bear these cheerfully, the apostle reminds them of what Christ has done for men. Nothing so soon reconciles Christians to the trials laid upon them as this.

In interpreting the words before us, it is necessary to realise and remember the object which the apostle had in view when he wrote them. No exposition can be correct which does not make this object prominent, and of which this object does not form the animating soul. We say this all the more confidently, when we observe that the apostle, after writing this controverted passage, which, properly speaking, extends to the end of the chapter, resumes his exhortation by saying in the first verse of next chapter, "Forasmuch then as Christ has suffered because of the flesh, arm yourselves likewise with the same mind," or thought, or purpose. These words seem to leave no room for doubting that all between them and the beginning of our text bears on the same point. In this verse (iv. 1) he commences a new branch of his exhortation, though in the same general strain.

Ver. 18a. *"Ὅτι καὶ Χριστὸς ἅπαξ περὶ ἁμαρτιῶν ἔπαθε*—" *Because Christ also suffered for sins once.*" The Revisers of 1881 tell us that many ancient authorities read *died* instead of *suffered*. This reading in no way affects the sense, but it serves as a kind of commentary, for the meaning evidently is that Christ *suffered unto death* for sins. This clause describes the penal character of Christ's sufferings. He bore on the cross the consequences of man's transgressions. Sin is the cause of all suffering. Had our first parents remained sinless we would have been exempt, it may be supposed, from all pain and sorrow. And Christ would not have required to assume our nature, and endure the accursed death of the cross.

Ver. 18b. *Δίκαιος ὑπὲρ ἀδίκων*—" *The righteous for the unrighteous.*" This clause describes the vicarious character of Christ's sufferings. He had no sin of His own, but, having become man's substitute, He suffered in his stead. He was dealt with as if He had been a sinner. The perfect spotlessness of Christ makes a world-wide difference between Him and mere men. There seems nothing peculiar in mere men suffering, for transgression and punishment are naturally associated. The wonderful thing is to see a sinless being enduring suffering. O the love of Christ, that could induce Him, though in no sense liable to punishment for personal acts, to endure the penalty of sin in our stead!

Ver. 18c. *"Ἵνα ἡμᾶς προσαγάγῃ τῷ Θεῷ*—" *That He might bring us to God.*" This clause expresses the ultimate object aimed at by the sufferings of Christ. (1) Christ died *to secure for us forgiveness with God.* The existence of sin is the great bar in the way of communion and confiding friendship with God. When we know that sin is forgiven we can look towards Him without alarm. Christ's death secures the forgiveness of all who put their trust in His atoning sacrifice. He fully satisfied the demands of the divine law, and rendered it possible for God to be just while justifying him who believeth in Jesus. (2) Christ died *to reconcile us to God*, to take away the enmity of our hearts against Him. The sinner naturally hates God, and continues to do so till he sees how his sin may be put away. The death of Christ is the great means employed by God to subdue the sinner's opposition to Him. The love manifested in the cross melts the hard and impenitent heart, and makes men love Him who first loved them. (3) Christ died *to prepare us for fellowship with God*. The sanctification of the believer, as well as his justification, springs from Christ's atoning death. The Bible tells us of the covenant made in His blood; and it is through the truth of the Bible and by the Spirit that we are sanctified. The Holy Spirit uses the word for the purification of our spirits; but if Christ had not died, neither the word nor the Holy Spirit would have been given.

But how Christ by His death brings us to God, the apostle explains in the next clause, which is expository or epexegetical of that on which we have just been commenting. And it is interesting to notice that the four clauses of this verse go in pairs, and explain each other. The second clause explains the first, and shows how Christ was called upon to endure suffering; the fourth, as we have said, explains the third, and shows how Christ brings men to God.

Ver. 18*d*. Θανατωθεὶς μὲν σαρκὶ, ζωοποιηθεὶς δὲ πνεύματι—" *Put to death because of the flesh, but restored* *to life because of the spirit.*" The nouns *flesh* and *spirit* stand, in the Greek, in the dative case, without any preposition before them. In translating into English it is necessary to supply one. What shall it be? The version of 1611 uses *in* before *flesh* and *by* before *spirit*. Modern scholars condemn this as grammatically unsound, and say that whatever preposition, or prepositional phrase, we use in the one case we must use also in the other. Carrying out this theory, the Revisers of 1881 use *in* before both nouns. We venture to call this theory in question. Its soundness would have been unimpeachable, if it had been certain that both datives are of the same character. As we regard them, this is not so. We have here a double clause, the two members of which are contrasted, as the particles μέν—δέ indicate. And the construction and translation depend entirely upon the light in which we view these two members, and particularly the two nouns which they contain. We take σαρκί as a *dativus incommodi* and πνεύματι as a *dativus commodi*. The true nature of these two datives has not been perceived by interpreters; hence they have failed to understand the passage. Such datives are not uncommon in the New Testament. Winer gives us the following examples. (1) Of *dativi incommodi*, Matt. xxiii. 31, "Ώστε μαρτυρεῖτε ἑαυτοῖς ὅτι υἱοί ἐστε τῶν φονευσάντων τοὺς προφήτας—" Wherefore ye witness to (or against) yourselves that ye are the sons of them that slew the prophets." Jas. v. 3, Ὁ χρυσὸς ὑμῶν, καὶ ὁ ἄργυρος κατίωται, καὶ ὁ ἰὸς αὐτῶν εἰς μαρτύριον ὑμῖν ἔσται—"Your gold and silver are rusted; and their rust shall be a testimony against you." Heb. vi. 6, Ἀνασταυροῦντας ἑαυτοῖς τὸν υἱὸν τοῦ Θεοῦ—" Seeing they crucify to themselves the son of God afresh." Rom. xiii. 2, Οἱ δὲ ἀνθεστηκότες ἑαυτοῖς κρῖμα λήψονται—"And they that withstand shall receive to themselves judgment." (2) Of *dativi commodi*. John iii. 26, ᾯ σὺ μεμαρτύρηκας—"To whom thou barest witness." Luke iv. 22, Καὶ πάντες ἐμαρτύρουν αὐτῷ—"And all bare Him witness." Rom x. 2, Μαρτυρῶ γὰρ αὐτοῖς—"For I bear them witness." 2 Cor. ii. 1, Ἔκρινα δὲ ἐμαυτῷ τοῦτο—"But I determined this for myself." The use of such datives by the sacred writers cannot therefore be disputed. In fact, many such datives are used by the sacred penmen. The only peculiarity in this case is that here *in this double clause* we assert that we have both a *dativus incommodi* and a *dativus commodi*. But can that be any argument against the view we take? If they occur separately, what hinders that they should occur together? There is no other case in the New Testament, so far as we know, where such an example of their conjunction occurs; but neither is that any argument against our view. In translation we might have used in the one instance the preposition *against* and in the other *for*. These really express the meaning. But such a translation might not be considered very elegant English. And so we fall back upon the longer and more colourless prepositional expression, and try to bring out the difference in our exposition. We may add that in Rom. iv. 25 we have a similar thought to that expressed, in this clause, though the grammatical form is different. "Ὃς παρεδόθη διὰ τὰ παραπτώματα ἡμῶν, καὶ ἠγέρθη διὰ τὴν δικαίωσιν ἡμῶν—"Who was delivered for our offences, and was raised for our justification." Compare also 1 Cor. v. 5, where there is a somewhat similar thought with again a different grammatical form.

It is hardly necessary, in these days, to expose the inaccuracy of the rendering of this double clause in the version of 1611. But that rendering will not bear a close examination. *Being put to death in the flesh* seems strangely unsuitable language to apply to Christ. It would seem to imply that something else than His body died. It does not really express the death of His body at all, though those unaccustomed to the accurate use of language may think it strange that we should say so. This part of our text, as it stands in our authorised translation, strictly and grammatically means that Christ in some sense died while in the flesh, that is, while still living. A translation of a portion of Scripture involving such a contradiction as this cannot be accurate. If Peter's desire was to convey the idea that Christ died, what need was there for the words *in the flesh*? *Quickened by the Spirit* is a translation equally objectionable, but for a different reason. It makes the Holy Spirit the agent in our Lord's resurrection. This is clear from their writing the word Spirit with a capital letter. Such an idea occurs nowhere else in Scripture. The Father is spoken of as raising up Christ from the dead, and He is spoken of as rising Himself; but this work is never ascribed to the Holy Spirit.

Our rendering is exposed to no such objections. It complies with the rules of Greek syntax, and, as we shall see, brings out a scriptural and consistent sense. But the apostle happily delivers us from all possibility of doubt as to the proper preposition to employ. He has put on record proof that he uses the two words *flesh* and *spirit* as *expressive of intention or purpose,* which everyone in the slightest degree acquainted with the peculiarities of Greek grammar is aware may be translated by such a phrase as we have used. The evidence that the apostle uses the two words referred to in the way we have already mentioned is very clear and convincing. That evidence we find in the 1st verse of the fourth chapter of this Epistle, which we have already quoted—"Forasmuch then as Christ has suffered because of the flesh, arm yourselves likewise with the same purpose"—ἔννοιαν. The Revisers use the term *mind* and put in the margin *thought*. But whatever word we employ the essential idea is the same.—It is to be observed that the apostle in the first clause of this verse (iv. 1) reduplicates upon the first half of that clause, the meaning of which we are now seeking to determine. He uses the word *flesh* in the same way as it is employed in that clause. Now, we think there cannot be any doubt that he uses it to express a purpose. How otherwise could he say, "Arm yourselves likewise with the *same mind,*" or *thought*, or *purpose*? These words can have no relevance unless you suppose the first clause to express a purpose. And how can it be viewed as doing so, if you translate in any other way than as we have done? We shall by and by speak of this purpose, but meanwhile our business is with the correct translation of the apostle's words.

This double clause, the translation of which we have thus determined, contains, as we apprehend, the greatest difficulty in connection with this long-controverted passage. The interpretation of this clause once settled, all else will be found to be comparatively simple. Our translation puts its teaching in a different light from that of any previous exposition, so far as we know. No one accepting our translation could ever conclude that *flesh* and *spirit* apply to

Christ. They must apply to men. In this respect, which is certainly a very vital one, our interpretation is new. Had interpreters sought to expound the clause in the direction of our translation, the whole difficulties of the passage would have disappeared long ago. But, persisting as they have done in applying the words *flesh* and *spirit* to Christ, it is not to be wondered at that their expositions have proved unsatisfactory. The clause bears on the face of it evidence that the words referred to were never meant to apply to Christ. It is a participial and parenthetical clause, added, as we have already observed, to explain how men are brought to God. It is therefore a distorting of it from its plain intention to regard all its meaning as absorbed in a reference to Christ.

The words *flesh* and *spirit* as applied to men are capable of two explanations. (1) In the first place, they may be understood as denoting the two great parts of human nature, the material and the spiritual. The following passages are examples of such a use of the words :—" The *spirit* indeed is willing, but the *flesh* is weak."[1] "To deliver such a one unto Satan for the destruction of the *flesh*, that the *spirit* may be saved in the day of the Lord Jesus."[2] (2) In the second place, they may be understood as denoting man's *corrupt* and *renewed natures* respectively. The following passages furnish examples of such a use of the words :—"For they that are after the *flesh* do mind the things of the *flesh*; but they that are after the *spirit* the things of the spirit."[3] "For he that soweth to his own *flesh* shall of the *flesh* reap corruption, but he that soweth unto the *spirit* shall of the *spirit* reap eternal life."[4] "But ye are not in the

[1] Matt. xxvi. 41.   [2] 1 Cor. v. 5.   [3] Rom. viii. 5.   [4] Gal. vi. 8.

*flesh*, but in the *spirit*; if so be that the Spirit of God dwelleth in you."[1] "But I say, Walk by the *spirit*, and ye shall not fulfil the lust of the *flesh*. For the *flesh* lusteth against the *spirit*, and the *spirit* against the *flesh*: for these are contrary the one to the other."[2] Some may be inclined to hesitate before admitting that the word *spirit* in these passages, where written with a small initial letter, means *the renewed nature of man*. Many such passages as those we have quoted are read by some with a kind of confused idea that the word means the Holy Spirit. The way in which it is contrasted with *flesh*, however, shows that the sense which we have attached to it is the correct one. The passages which we have quoted become much more intelligible when we so interpret it. But we do not wish to delay the reader by any further defence of this meaning of the word *spirit*. All good interpreters admit that the words *flesh* and *spirit* are used in the New Testament in the manner we are now insisting on. And this is enough for our purpose.

The second explanation of the words *flesh* and *spirit*, that, namely, which regards them as denoting *man's corrupt* and *renewed natures*, is that which first presented itself to our mind after we had determined the translation of the clause in which they occur. And all our subsequent study has tended to deepen our conviction of the accuracy of this view. The tenor of the two parts of the clause indicates with sufficient clearness how the purpose is to be formulated in either case. Besides, we have the apostle's own words to guide us to the first half of the clause, as we have seen. In ch. iv. 1, 2 we read, "Forasmuch, then, as Christ

[1] Rom. viii. 9.      [2] Gal. v. 16, 17.

has suffered because of the flesh, arm yourselves likewise with the same purpose (or mind, or thought) —for he that hath suffered because of the flesh hath ceased from sin,[1]—with the view no longer to live the rest of your time in the flesh to the lusts of men, but to the will of God." We have translated from the text of Westcott and Hort. The last part of this quotation furnishes the explanation of the *purpose* mentioned in the first part. That purpose is the mortification of man's *corrupt* nature. It is to this that the believers to whom Peter wrote the Epistle were exhorted. As Christ suffered for the *same purpose*, the apostle's words indicate the proper formulæ to be employed in our exposition of the clause now before us.

1. Christ was put to death *for the conquest and destruction of the corrupt nature of man.* In one of its

---

[1] This clause, which we have punctuated with dashes, is evidently parenthetical. It is meant to strengthen the exhortation which the apostle addresses to his readers, to arm themselves with the same purpose which Christ had in view in suffering. He is in haste to state that purpose, as it ought to take shape in the minds of his readers. He is hurrying on with his old natural impetuosity, and he throws out this hint as it were just by the way. The idea is that if his readers will obey his exhortation they will reach entire deliverance from sin. Let them look to Christ their great pattern. He once had connexion with sin as our substitute, but He has no longer such a connexion. He has obtained the reward consequent upon the carrying out of His purpose. He is now in glory, far beyond all the sufferings and sorrows of earth. To the same blessed reward and enjoyment all who obey the exhortation of the apostle will attain. It is significant that Christ is not here said to have died to sin; He was never alive to it. His connexion with it was as a sufferer, but that connexion has now ceased. Mere men do not cease from sin till they are admitted to glory. While here they are imperfect, and exposed to suffering. The *privilege* of perfect deliverance from sin and all its consequences is the great encouragement which the apostle holds out to his readers to carry out in their lives the same *purpose* which Christ had in His sufferings.

aspects the great change which takes place in man at conversion is called a *death*. It is a death to sin. His past life of disobedience to God is regarded as a thing with which he has no more connexion than a dead man has with this life. The figure is very expressive, for, of course, the language is not literal, but figurative. If the language were anything but figurative, we would expect converted men to be perfectly holy. One of the great purposes for which Christ died was to lead men to die to sin, in order to their being brought to God. Christ's death is operative upon the believer to this end at the time of his conversion, but it continues to be so also during his whole life on earth. He dies daily unto sin as well as becomes dead to it when he is born again. Nothing can destroy sin in man but the death of Christ. It is the exhibition of Christ, and particularly of His atoning death, to the soul, which leads a man to mortify the flesh with its affections and lusts. "For what the law could not do in that it was weak through the flesh, God, sending His own Son in the likeness of sinful flesh, and for sin, condemned sin in the flesh, that the ordinance of the law might be fulfilled in us who walk not after the flesh, but after the spirit."[1]

2. Christ was made alive *for the vivification and enfranchisement of the renewed nature of man.* The accuracy of this formula follows as a necessary consequence from that suggested by the apostle for the exposition of the first part of the clause now before us. The change which takes place in the sinner at conversion has a twofold aspect, a negative and a positive. The one aspect is related ethically to the death of Christ, the other ethically to His resurrec-

[1] Rom. viii. 3.

tion. As the sinner dies to sin, so he becomes alive to righteousness. This twofold aspect of conversion helps to explain such a verse as, "Testifying both to Jews and to Greeks, repentance toward God, and faith toward our Lord Jesus Christ."[1] That one of the purposes of Christ's resurrection was to lead men to a new life, the Scriptures abundantly testify. "We were buried with Him through baptism into death, that like as Christ was raised from the dead through the glory of the Father, so we also might walk in newness of life."[2] "Buried with Christ in baptism, wherein ye were also raised with Him through faith in the working of God, who raised Him from the dead."[3] As there is a power in connexion with the death of Christ to lead to the mortification of the flesh, so there is a power in connexion with the resurrection of Christ to lead to the vivification of the spirit. And as the power of Christ's death is felt, not only at conversion, but also throughout the whole of the believer's life, so the power of Christ's resurrection is felt during the whole of the believer's pilgrimage here.

That the ethical relations of Christ's death and resurrection are such as we have described, the Epistles everywhere attest. In addition to the passages already quoted, we may adduce the following:—"If ye died with Christ from the rudiments of the world, why, as though living in the world, do ye subject yourselves to ordinances?"[4] "If ye then were raised together with Christ, seek the things that are above, where Christ is, seated on the right hand of God."[5] "For if we have become united with Him

---

[1] Acts xx. 21.  [2] Rom. vi. 4.  [3] Col. ii. 12.
[4] Col. ii. 20.  [5] Col. iii. 1.

by the likeness of His death, we shall be also by the likeness of His resurrection; knowing this, that our old man was crucified with Him, that the body of sin might be done away, that so we should no longer be in bondage to sin."[1]

In the relations of which we are speaking, we have, as we have pointed out, an exhibition of the ethical effects of Christ's work for men. We see how that work influences the mind, and draws men to the acceptance of its benefits. This feature of the mediatorial work of Christ is different from that on which we generally dwell, namely, its sacrificial character. In the preceding clauses of this verse the apostle has been speaking of Christ's work as a sacrifice made to God's justice, so that men might be brought to God. We see the process of bringing men to God in the moral influences of the atonement exhibited in the double clause at present before us. And this clause naturally follows the others. Satisfaction must be rendered to God's law by Christ's work before men can be affected by it. This view of the matter is borne out by the evidently explanatory nature of this clause. It bears on the face of it that it is added to throw some additional light on what has gone before.[2]

[1] Rom. vi. 5.
[2] Ch. iv. 6 has always been felt to be a difficult passage. As its phraseology closely resembles that of the clause now under consideration, we are compelled to look at it with some care. It uses the words *flesh* and *spirit* in the same way as they are used in that clause. We render it thus: "For, for this reason was the gospel preached also to them that are dead, that they might be judged after the manner of men because of the flesh, but might live in a Godlike manner because of the spirit." In the 5th verse the apostle seeks to encourage his readers in the pursuit of holiness by the consideration that Christ will on the great day judge all men, as well those who

The exposition which we have now given of this verse invests it with a unity and consistency which it does not possess when otherwise viewed. The great design of the verse is to point out the purpose of shall then have died as those who shall then be found alive. The great test on the great day for those who have heard the gospel will be the way in which they have treated it. Hence the apostle is led to declare in the 6th verse that all such who have already died had the gospel preached to them to prepare them for the great day. Of course the apostle's words are to be understood as having reference only to whose who have heard the gospel. The heathen, who have never heard the joyful sound, will be tried by a different standard from that used in the case of those who have enjoyed a revelation of the divine will.

The preaching of the gospel institutes, as it were, a preliminary trial. The reception or rejection of it will determine the sentence pronounced on that day. God mercifully seeks to prepare men for the judgment day by offering them mercy through Christ, and seeking to induce them to live as becomes the gospel. The apostle illustrates this by the case of those who had heard the gospel in the past, but were now dead.

1. The gospel was preached to those who were then dead, that they might be judged as men, that is, as sinners. It examines the state of men's hearts, and lays bare all the impurity and sin which lurk there. It puts a man through a process similar to that which he undergoes when he is tried in a court of law, and it finds him guilty. Then it sentences the flesh to death. The corrupt nature must be mortified and destroyed. The word *judged* then expresses both the sifting and condemnatory offices of the gospel. The word is beautifully appropriate.

2. But the gospel performs another function in men besides those mentioned. It condemns the flesh—the old nature, to destruction, but it gives us also a new nature. It kills, but it also gives life. And this life is according to the divine pattern. It is a life of holiness—like God's. The purpose for which the gospel is preached is not fulfilled in man unless this result is secured. The new nature with its impulses prompting us to live in a Godlike manner is imparted to us to lead us to life in the spirit,—that holy obedience and purity which the word *spirit* as opposed to *flesh* implies. The idea of the last clause of this verse is clearly seen when we speak of the *life in a Godlike manner as the new nature*, and *the spirit* as the manifestation of that new nature.

Christ's mediatorial work, namely, to bring men to God. The last clause shows how by the ethical influences of His death and resurrection He accomplishes this. Our exposition, if correct, strikes at the root of all the speculations in which men have indulged, in connection with this passage, about what Christ did in His disembodied state. The verse, as we view it, is silent about Christ's state or action between His death and resurrection.

But our exposition of this verse is not complete till we animate it with the spirit of the apostle's purpose in writing the passage. That purpose was to lead his readers to a patient endurance of the sufferings to which they were subjected. Now, how admirably does this verse further this purpose! If Christ suffered all that He did endure, though innocent, for us, should we not be ready to suffer for Him? It is one of the most incumbent duties of Christians to bear suffering even unto death for His sake, if necessary. Then, we are brethren of Christ and devoted to His interests: should we not be willing to suffer if, through our sufferings, others may be led to God? We may well do so, since the sufferings which Christ endured have secured for us exemption from all pain in the world to come.

The late Dr. John Brown, of Edinburgh, in his Expository Discourses on this Epistle, translates the last half of the clause of this verse, "being quickened in the spirit," which he interprets to mean *quickened spiritually*.[1] "A consequence," says he, "of our Lord's penal, vicarious, expiatory sufferings was, that

---

[1] We quote his words because he is a good example of a certain class of expositors. And quite recently in *The Expository Times*, a prominent Edinburgh clergyman has warmly endorsed Dr. Brown's view.

He became spiritually alive and powerful in a sense and to a degree in which He was not previously, and in which, but for these sufferings, He never would have become—full of life to be communicated to dead souls, mighty to save." This at first sight seems beautifully ingenious; but, unfortunately for its soundness, the word translated in our Authorised Version of the passage, *quickened*, never means, in the New Testament, *having a larger measure of life communicated*. Wherever it occurs in the New Testament it means *made alive*, and refers either to the communication or restoration of natural life, or to the communication of spiritual life—the implantation of the new nature. The word *quickened* does mean in the English language what Dr. Brown's view requires; but when such a sense is attached to it, it is not a correct translation of the Greek word used in the New Testament. It would be easy to prove this if it were necessary. But let us suppose, for the sake of argument, that the word has, in this passage, the meaning for which Dr. Brown contends. Christ must have been quickened either in His divine or in His human nature. Dr. Brown does not mean in His divine nature, for he pronounces such an idea " obviously absurd and false, as implying that He who is 'the life,' the living one, can be quickened either in the sense of, restored from a state of death, or endowed with a larger measure of vitality." He must mean, therefore, that it was Christ's human nature that was quickened. But here the objection comes in with unanswerable force, that Christ does not, as man, but as God, bestow eternal blessings upon men. It is as God-man that He bestows upon us repentance and forgiveness.

These remarks just made dispose of the view of those who think the last clause of this verse teaches that Christ's body was put to death while His spirit *was kept alive*. The Greek word, ζωοποιέω, has never in the New Testament this meaning. And the passage cited from the Septuagint in Poole's *Synopsis* —1 Sam. xxvii. 9—to prove that it means there to *keep alive*, does not contain the word at all, but ζωογονέω. But even though fifty passages could be named in which ζωοποιέω might be alleged or proved to mean *to keep alive*, this would not meet the difficulty that the contrast in the clause before us renders such a sense inadmissible here. Such a sense attached to the word would imply the possibility of Christ's spirit being put to death—an idea which is certainly incorrect, whether we make the possibility apply to our Lord's human soul or to His divine nature. But we have already shown that every view which refers the words *flesh* and *spirit* to Christ is made inadmissible by the language of the apostle. We need not therefore argue further against such views. Turn we now to the next verse.

Ver. 19a. Ἐν ᾧ καὶ τοῖς ἐν φυλακῇ πνεύμασι πορευθεὶς ἐκήρυξεν—" *Wherefore* (literally, *In which*) *He even went and preached to the spirits in prison.*" The first point requiring our attention here is the expression *in which*, which we translate freely *wherefore*. What is the antecedent to which? To what does it refer? It is a question of grammar; and in dealing with such a point we must take the literal, not the free translation. Those who take a certain view of the passage say that *spirit*, in the preceding verse, is the antecedent to *which*. And we are told that, by the inexorable laws of grammar, we can come to no other conclusion. This is the great argument in favour of the view that Christ in His disembodied spirit preached to disembodied spirits. This view rests on the assumption that *spirit* in the preceding verse means Christ's *disembodied spirit*. We trust our exposition of that verse proves that this is by no means self-evident, nay, that it is utterly inadmissible. But even supposing that the word *spirit* had the meaning alleged, we deny that the laws of grammar would render it necessary that we take *spirit* as the antecedent to *which*. The antecedent to a relative is sometimes to be gathered out of a preceding sentence or statement. Of this the Apostle Paul's words in the Epistle to the Galatians furnish a remarkable example: "For it is written, that Abraham had two sons; the one by a bond maid, and the other by a free woman. But he who was of the bond woman was born after the flesh; but he of the free woman was by promise—*which things* are an allegory." The relative here is compound, but this does not affect its value as a grammatical example in point. This is the rule which applies in the present case. It is the object which Christ had in view in dying, namely, to bring men to God, which is the antecedent to the relative *which*: *in which object*, that is, with which object in view, He even went and preached to the spirits in prison. Every scholar knows that there are hundreds of examples in classical writers of relatives referring, not to the nearest word, but to a whole clause.

The interpretation which we have just given to the expression under consideration is a corollary from our exposition of the preceding verse. And from the way in which we have grounded that exposition, we would be perfectly warranted in holding that the expression now before us can be interpreted only in the manner we have just mentioned. But we have no desire to give ourselves even the appearance of dogmatising on any point. Can we gather no principle for our guidance out of the manner in which the apostle uses the expression elsewhere? Every writer has his favourite expressions, which he often uses in some particular way. We call this a peculiarity of style. Now, the apostle uses this expression in other three passages of this Epistle outside of our text: it does not occur in his Second Epistle at all. He has thus given us sufficient means of observing whether he uses it in any peculiar way. We shall be able to show that *he never uses it in such a way as to make the immediately preceding noun the antecedent to 'which.'* To put the matter in another form, to bring out the full meaning of the expression *in which* as used by Peter, we must supply *matter, object, concern, thing,* or some such word —terms, in short, corresponding to the Greek χρῆμα and the Latin *negotium* or *res.* If we can prove this, everyone can see how powerfully it will confirm our interpretation of the preceding verse, and how strongly it will militate against the view of those who think *spirit* in the preceding verse is the antecedent to *which.* We shall take the passages in which the expression occurs in the order in which they are found in the Epistle.

1. The first example is in ch. i. 6, where the expression is rendered in our Authorised Version, and in the Revision as well, *wherein.* To make the matter clear, it is necessary to quote the context: " Blessed be the God and Father of our Lord Jesus Christ, who, according to His great mercy, begat us again unto a living hope, by the resurrection of Jesus Christ from the dead, unto an inheritance incorruptible, and unde-

filed, and that fadeth not away, reserved in heaven for you, who by the power of God are guarded through faith unto a salvation, ready to be revealed in the last time, wherein (*literally*, in which) ye greatly rejoice, though now for a season, if need be, ye are in heaviness through manifold temptations." The question to be determined here is this: Is the antecedent to *which* the immediately preceding word *time*, or the whole matter of the preceding context which we have quoted? Against the former alternative there occurs the damaging objection that men cannot be said to rejoice in what is still in the future. They may rejoice in the hope of it, but this is not what the apostle affirms. And the word *rejoice* is in the present tense; it is not *will rejoice*. To meet this difficulty, we are told that the present tense is used here in the sense of the future. But does not such a principle as this, resorted to at pleasure, tend to throw an air of uncertainty around the whole word of God? If we interpret this passage by such a principle, why not others? Give us leave to use such a licentious principle, and we undertake to overthrow the most precious teachings of the Bible. We are therefore compelled to adopt the latter alternative of our question, and to conclude that the antecedent to *which* is to be gathered out of the preceding context which we have quoted. The apostle is there speaking of some of the privileges of God's people. These he gathers all together into a unity in the expression under consideration, and views them as one *matter*— "in which matter ye greatly rejoice," etc. Is not such a peculiarity of style the dashing, impetuous Peter all over? for, as has been observed, a man's style is himself. The rejoicing which the apostle ascribes to his readers is not inconsistent with temporary depression and sorrow. He is speaking of what is habitual with all God's people, not of what is merely casual. The believer habitually rejoices in his privileges, though he may experience occasional distress. The child of God has every reason for being a happy man, though he may at times be overwhelmed with grief and gloom.

2. The second example of the apostle's use of the expression before us occurs in ch. ii. 12, where it is translated in our Authorised Version *whereas*, and in the Revision *wherein*. As before, we quote the context: "Dearly beloved, I beseech you, as strangers and pilgrims, to abstain from fleshly lusts, which war against the soul; having your behaviour honest among the Gentiles: that, wherein (*literally*, in which or what) they speak against you as evil-doers, they may by your good works, which they behold, glorify God in the day of visitation." There can be no question here that the antecedent to *which* or *what* is not any word in the preceding context. No interpreter has ever maintained that such an antecedent can be found. The antecedent is to be gathered out of the preceding context. And it is to be found in the matter of conduct there referred to. Peter is exhorting his readers to continue to cultivate a holy life, so that, *in what respect*, or *in that respect in which* their enemies spoke against them as evil-doers (because, as the apostle, as we shall see, elsewhere affirms, the Christians would not run riot in every kind of iniquity with their heathen fellow-men), they might, by their good works, glorify God in the day of visitation. Those who were now opposed to them would see their good works and glorify their Father in heaven.

3. The third and last example, beyond our text, of the apostle's use of the expression referred to is found in ch. iv. 4, where it is translated in both versions *wherein*. We quote the context as before: " For the time past may suffice to have wrought the desire of the Gentiles, and to have walked in lasciviousness, lusts, wine - bibbings, revellings, carousings, and abominable idolatries, wherein (*literally*, in which) they think it strange that you run not with them into the same excess of riot, speaking evil of you." Here again the antecedent to *which* cannot be any word in the preceding context. The immediately preceding word is in the *plural* number, whereas *which* is in the *singular*. We must gather the antecedent, therefore, from the general sense of what goes before. That refers again to the matter of conduct. The apostle gathers together into a unity all the different features of conduct there mentioned, and says, "*in which, that is, in which matter of conduct*, they think it strange," etc.

These three examples of the apostle's use of the expression under consideration furnish, apart altogether from our interpretation of the preceding verse, a strong presumption, to say the very least, that he uses it according to the same principle in this 19th verse, and that *spirit* in the 18th verse is not the antecedent to *which* in this.

The conjunction *even* (καί) tallies with this explanation of the expression under consideration, and confirms it. When we read of Christ *even* having gone and preached to the spirits in prison, we are forced to infer that He has been represented as having done something else. We do not find this inference satisfied by the statement that Christ was quickened *in* the spirit or *by* the spirit. The verb there is passive, representing Christ as having had something done to Him, not as having done something, as the inference requires. We are carried away back, therefore, to the statement that Christ died to bring men to God. This meets the necessities of the case. Christ died to bring men to God: with the same object in view He *even* went and preached to the spirits in prison.

But we must now say a few words on the accuracy of our free translation of the expression under consideration. Here our object will be gained by quoting a passage in which the expression occurs in the sense which we have assigned to it. Thus we find in Heb. vi. 17, "For men swear by the greater; and in every dispute of theirs an oath is final for confirmation. Wherefore (*literally*, in which) God, being minded to show more abundantly unto the heirs of the promise the immutability of His counsel, interposed with an oath." Here clearly the expression can mean only what we have rendered it in our free translation. This sense of the expression is not frequent, but it is enough that we can point to one passage where it occurs—a passage in which Winer says it is used in the sense we have assigned to it.

The next question to be considered is, who were the *spirits in prison* to whom Christ preached? The answers which have been given to this question naturally range themselves into two classes. (1) The Roman Catholic one, which has been adopted, with certain modifications, by many Protestants. This answer is that Christ went after His death, and in His disembodied state, and preached to disembodied spirits who had not committed mortal sin, but were at that time in prison in Purgatory. This answer, with all its Protestant modifications, goes directly in the face of that great truth lying upon the surface of the Bible throughout its whole extent, that after death there is no change in the relation which a man bears to God. "It is appointed unto men once to die, but after this the judgment."[1] "We must all be made manifest before the judgment-seat of Christ, that each one may receive the things done in the body, according to what he hath done, whether it be good or bad."[2] This doctrine is entirely superseded, if we are taught to believe that our eternal state after the final judgment will depend, not only upon the deeds done in the body, but upon those done by our disembodied spirits as well. If any man holds that Christ preached for their salvation to disembodied spirits who had not had the opportunity of receiving the truth in this world, he must hold, to be consistent, that there are others besides those to whom Christ preached who receive the offer of salvation after death, or show reason to the contrary. In short, such an idea opens the door to some of the wildest and most unscriptural dogmas of Romanism. If it be correct, then we are warranted to pray for the souls of the dead, that they may be enabled to receive the truth when it is presented to them in the intermediate state, for we cannot tell whether God will regard the light any one has enjoyed as having been sufficient for his conversion. And, as the probability is that the circumstances in which spirits will find themselves in another world will be more favourable for the reception of the truth than those in which they are placed here, with such an idea we have nothing to stop us from falling into universalism. But, besides, if it be true that sinners who have not had an opportunity

[1] Heb. ix. 27.        [2] 2 Cor. v. 10.

of embracing the gospel in time, will have such an opportunity afforded them after death, all motive to prosecute the missionary cause, or even to preach the gospel to the ignorant among us, is taken away. Nay, must not the preaching of the gospel to any man be regarded as cruelty? Better far that we all remained ignorant of it, if we are to have the offer of it in another state, which will in all probability be more favourable to our reception of it.

Bishop Horsley is one of the most prominent Protestant theologians who have adopted a modification of the Roman Catholic view. His interpretation claims special notice, not only because of his great learning, but also because of the influence which he has exercised over subsequent theological writers. That interpretation we find in a sermon on the passage we are now considering. The object of the sermon is to vindicate the clause in the so-called Apostles' Creed which speaks of our Lord's descent into hell. This descent we are told was "an action performed by Him after He was dead and buried, and before He rose again." Hell, we are further told, "must be some place below the surface of the earth." Calvin's idea, that our Lord descended to the place of torment, is rejected with horror. "The word (hell), in its natural import, signifies only that invisible place which is the appointed habitation of departed souls in the interval between death and the general resurrection." The New Testament writers "divide this central mansion of the dead into two distinct regions, for the separate lodging of the souls of the righteous and the reprobate." "He (Christ) descended to hell, properly so called,—to the invisible mansions of departed spirits, and to that part of it where the souls of the faithful, when they are delivered from the burden of the flesh, are in joy and felicity." Such, in brief, and in his own words, is Horsley's interpretation of the clause in the so-called Apostles' Creed. He then proceeds to support this interpretation by a reference to certain texts of Scripture. And these texts he strives, with no doubt the most honest intention, to bend to his purpose.

He cites, first, our Lord's words to the penitent robber, Lk. xxiii. 43, "To-day shalt thou be with Me in paradise." Paradise "was not heaven; for to heaven our Lord after His death ascended not till after His resurrection, as appears from His own words to Mary Magdalene." Paradise "could be no other than that region of repose and rest where the souls of the righteous abide in joyful hope of the consummation of their bliss."

Horsley's next proof text is the quotation which Peter made from the Psalmist on the day of Pentecost. Acts ii. 27, "Thou wilt not leave my soul in hell, neither wilt Thou suffer Thy Holy One to see corruption." His inference here is that Christ's soul must have been in hell.

The next proof adduced is Eph. iv. 9, "Now that He ascended, what is it but that He descended first into the lower parts of the earth." "This text," he says, "expressly affirms a descent of Christ's Spirit into hell."

Having thus carefully prepared his way, the good Bishop turns with some degree of confidence to the words of our apostle. He says Peter's meaning turns on the sense we assign to the phrase *the spirits in prison*. He translates the clause in which the phrase occurs thus: "He went and preached to the spirits *in safe keeping."* He thinks Peter means that Christ preached to the spirits in the interval between His death and resurrection. The exact rendering, therefore, of the apostle's words would be: "Being put to death in the flesh, but quick in the spirit"; that is, surviving in His soul the stroke of death which His body had sustained; "by which," or rather, "in which," that is, in which surviving soul, "He went and preached to the souls of men in prison, or in safe keeping."

To this view there are several obvious and serious objections—

1. It represents paradise as under the surface of the earth. The other two passages where the word occurs do not correspond with such an idea. Paul in 2 Cor. xii. speaks of being caught *up* into paradise. In Rev. ii. 7 we read, "To him that overcometh will I give to eat of the tree of life which is in the midst of the paradise of God." Is that consistent with the learned Bishop's view? Is it a thing to be desired that we be sent, after overcoming, to a place of safe keeping under ground? Is the tree of life there? Is the paradise of God there?

2. The passages which Horsley adduces about Christ descending to the lower parts of the earth simply mean that He died and entered into the state of the dead. The same is true of the quotation from the Psalmist which Peter makes. Christ did not remain in the state of the dead till His body underwent decomposition.

3. The word *quick*, or living, is not a correct rendering of the original Greek term ζωοποιηθείς. *Made alive* or *restored to life* is the only possible translation. This is clear from the contrast stated in the clause. Christ was put to death by wicked men, but was

restored to life by the Father. The Greek word for *quick* is ζῶν. The term occurs in 2 Tim. iv. 1 and in 1 Pet. iv. 5, where, in both cases, it is contrasted with νεκρός.

4. The idea of Christ preaching to the spirits *in safe keeping* between His death and resurrection is excluded from the passage by the fact that His preaching is not mentioned till after His resurrection. For, of course, as we have just pointed out, the word ζωοποιηθείς refers to our Lord's resurrection.

There are other objections which might have been stated to this view, but we have said enough to show that it is untenable. Notwithstanding, however, the glaring objections to which it is exposed, it is largely accepted in the present day. Among those who adhere to it are men like the late Dean Plumptre and the present Dean of Canterbury, Dr. Farrar.

Those who take *spirit* in ver. 18 to mean Christ's *disembodied spirit*, seem to think that the close connexion between vv. 18 and 19 renders it necessary to conclude He preached to disembodied spirits. His preaching is mentioned after His death. But it is overlooked that it is mentioned also after His resurrection. Many minds seem to become confused here. If we keep in view the apostle's purpose in writing this passage, we shall see that the connexion between vv. 18 and 19 is not chronological, but logical The fact that Christ's preaching, in the case under consideration, is mentioned after His death and resurrection, can be accounted for on the ground that it supplies one of the best illustrations which the apostle could give of Christ's desire to bring men to God. He was not required to give His illustrations of such a point in the chronological order. Nay, the order

He followed was that which any Christian going over the same ground might naturally follow. He began with the great means which Christ employed to bring men to God, and then spoke of another effort put forth, though used many ages before. The case of the antediluvians was special. It was necessary to take measures to separate the righteous from the wicked, otherwise the human race would have become extinct. No other such crisis has ever occurred in the history of the world calling for such special interference. That our Lord acted as He did at the time, shows how intensely He is in earnest in seeking to bring men to God. But we anticipate.

(2) The Protestant answer to the question, Who were the *spirits in prison* to whom Christ preached? is, that they were those who lived on the earth immediately before the Flood, and that Christ preached to them while they were in the flesh, and not after they died. This is our view. But why are they called *spirits*? It is hardly necessary to remark that we are not under any necessity to suppose that whenever this word occurs it means *disembodied spirits*. It has not this meaning in these passages, for example: "The grace of the Lord Jesus Christ be with your spirit."[1] "For who among men knoweth the things of a man, save the spirit of the man which is in him."[2] In our own language we call men *spirits*. We say such a man was the *master spirit* of his age, and we speak of turbulent men as *unruly spirits*. As the *spirit* is the most important part of man, it is naturally employed to describe the whole. We must not be astonished, therefore, to find the word so used by the apostle. He seems to have been prompted to

[1] Philem. 25.   [2] 1 Cor. ii. 11.

its use here by the remembrance of having used it in the preceding verse.

So far is the word *spirits* from necessarily meaning *disembodied spirits*, that, according to the Bible use of language, *spirits in prison* must be understood to mean *men in the flesh*. The following quotations seem to establish this:—" I the Lord have called thee in righteousness, and will hold thine hand, and will keep thee, and give thee for a covenant of the people, for a light of the Gentiles; to open the blind eyes, to bring out the prisoners from the prison, and them that sit in darkness out of the prison-house" (ἐξ οἴκου φυλακῆς).[1] "Bring my soul out of prison" (Ἐξάγαγε ἐκ φυλακῆς τὴν ψυχήν μου).[2] The Greek here quoted is that of the LXX., which, as everyone knows, has so largely influenced that of the New Testament. The allusion in these two passages is *not to disembodied spirits*, but to *men in the flesh*. This is so clear that we do not need to insist upon it. But another remark is suggested by these quotations. The word *prison* naturally gives rise to the thought that those who are confined in such a place are in danger. Some charge has been brought against, and they are more or less in peril. They may be in prison, previous to their execution. It needs no argument to show that some such idea is connected with both passages. The first evidently is a prediction concerning Christ. And the idea is that He is appointed to bring light and deliverance to those, whether Jews or Gentiles, who sit in the prison-house of darkness and sin. The words quoted from Ps. cxlii. are expressive of distress and the consciousness of danger. The Psalmist felt that from one cause or another his soul

[1] Isa. xlii. 7.      [2] Ps. cxlii. 7.

was in peril. We are therefore to infer that those spirits in prison to whom Christ is represented as having preached in the days of Noah are so described because their lives were in special danger. And it is not their bodies that are here regarded as in prison, but their spirits. Christ came, not to emancipate men's bodies, but their spirits. The spirit of man is, in a figurative sense, in prison; it is enthralled by sin. Those, therefore, referred to in the quotations which we have made from Isaiah and the Psalms are accurately described when we call them *spirits in prison*. And it would seem that Peter, in describing those who lived immediately before the Flood, borrowed his language from such passages as these. The expression, then, *spirits in prison*, describes the state of all men by nature. But there is an additional reason why those to whom Christ preached immediately before the Flood should be called *spirits in prison*. They are differentiated from other men by the character ascribed to them, and by the peculiar circumstances in which they were placed. They were under the special condemnation of God, and were like men condemned for a crime, and awaiting in prison their punishment; so that they were in a very special sense *spirits in prison*. This disposes of the view of those who understand Peter to mean that Christ preached to men *whose spirits are now in prison*.

An attempt has been made to prove that the expression, "the spirits in prison," means *Noah's family shut up in the ark*. This is a revival of the opinion first broached by Lord Barrington, the grandson of Caryl, the commentator on Job. It seems to find a kind of verbal warrant from 2 Pet. ii. 5, "If God spared not the old world, but kept in safety ($\dot{\epsilon}\phi\acute{u}\lambda a\xi\epsilon$)

Noah," etc. To understand the force of the argument founded upon this word, it is necessary to know that its cognate noun, φυλακῇ, is used in our text, and is translated *prison*. So that it seems the ark must be the prison spoken of in our text. But such a view is manifestly inadmissible. (1) Those to whom Christ preached are said to have been *disobedient* at the time of His preaching. This could not be affirmed of Noah's family, for they obeyed the divine warning, and found safety in the ark. (2) The apostle tells us Christ's preaching took place *while the ark was being prepared*, not after it was built. (3) The passage bears on the face of it that Noah's family were saved because they listened to the divine warning. But this view destroys all connection between the preaching and the preservation. (4) The apostle speaks of *few* being saved. This expression is evidently used in contrast to those who perished, who were *many*. A few believed the preaching, namely, Noah's family—many were disobedient.

The verb φυλάσσω and its cognate noun have different shades of meaning. They may be used of *a prison*, and be associated with the idea of trial and punishment; or they may be used of an *asylum of safety*. The same writer might, with propriety, use the words in the one sense at the one time, and in the other at another time. This is just what Peter has done. The context determines the sense.

The Unitarian version of the New Testament, published by the Socinians in 1808 to vindicate their heretical doctrines, has the following note on the passage before us: "He preached, not to the same individual persons, but to men like them, in the same circumstances; to the race of the Gentiles, to the descendants of those who had formerly been disobedient, and refused the call of the Spirit in Noah's time." As those who rejected the truth before the Flood were all swept away, it is difficult to see how they could have had any descendants.

But the question arises, How did He preach? in person? or, by proxy? Our Authorised translators seem to have had the idea that He preached through Noah by His Holy Spirit. But if our view of the passage be correct, the Holy Spirit is not referred to in it at all. We cannot resist the conclusion that the expression, "He went and preached," implies that in some sense He preached in person. This expression is like one which occurs in Eph. ii. 17, "He came and preached peace to you that were far off, and to them that were nigh." This passage is quoted to prove that His preaching in our text was not personal. But it is far from satisfactory as a proof of such a position. Nay, it proves the very reverse. He did come into the world and preach the gospel. The meaning of the passage is that He preached a gospel which was for Jews and Gentiles alike. No one contends that He preached to all men; but He personally preached a gospel which was for all men. "How shall we escape, if we neglect so great salvation; which having at the first been spoken by the Lord, was confirmed unto us by them that heard?"[1] Now, as the language in Ephesians so closely resembles the phraseology of that verse on which we are now commenting, and as it means that Christ personally preached peace, so our text must be interpreted to mean that He preached personally to the spirits in prison. If we can show that He preached personally

[1] Heb. ii. 3.

to Noah, this will be as much personal preaching to the spirits in prison as was His preaching while in the flesh, to them that were afar off, and to them that were nigh. If, then, we turn to Genesis and read the instructions which Noah received regarding the ark, we shall come to the conclusion that he received a personal visit from a divine person. Such visits were common in early patriarchal times. It is now a settled point among all sound divines that, on all such occasions, it was the Second Person of the Godhead who appeared — our Lord Jesus Christ. Christ, then, appeared to Noah, and warned him that the Flood was coming upon the world for its ungodliness. This was preaching personally, and for all then living. That Noah carried out the wishes of Christ, and made known to an ungodly world the communication which he had received, is evident from the fact that he is called by this same apostle "a preacher of righteousness." And this expression implies that he was not content with words of warning. He must have told his contemporaries of God's love and readiness to accept all workers of righteousness. It does not meet the requirements of the case to say merely that Christ preached by His Spirit. His preaching was directed towards "the spirits in prison" through Noah, as the words may be understood to mean, and Noah received the personal communication. So that the whole truth about Christ's preaching in Noah's time is, that He preached personally, first to Noah, and then through him to all men then living.

Ver. 20a. Those to whom Christ preached are described as "*at that time disobedient*" ($\dot{a}\pi\epsilon\iota\theta\dot{\eta}\sigma a\sigma\acute{\iota}$ $\pi o \tau \epsilon$). The expression refers to the time when the heavenly communication was made to them. They regarded the words of Noah as the outcome of a heated imagination. While he was preparing the ark, they would mock and insult him. They resembled that generation of Jews who lived when our Lord was incarnate. All generations of those to whom the gospel is preached, cannot be called *disobedient* in the same sense as those who lived immediately before the Flood; but, alas! the language is in some measure applicable to all men. The preaching of Christ in the days of Noah was, it seems, attended with small results.

Ver. 20b. "Ὅτε ἀπεξεδέχετο ἡ τοῦ Θεοῦ μακροθυμία, ἐν ἡμέραις Νῶε—" *When the long-suffering of God was continuing to wait in the days of Noah.*" God showed great patience with the antediluvians. He gave them special warning of the punishment which He was about to bring upon them in the event of their continuing impenitent. It is thought by some that the passage, "My Spirit shall not always strive with man, for he also is flesh: yet his days shall be an hundred and twenty years,"—it is thought that this passage expresses the length of time during which God continued to wait after the announcement made to Noah that He was about to bring a flood on the earth. If so, how remarkable was God's long-suffering, and what opportunities had the men of that time of fleeing from the wrath to come!

Ver. 20c. The time when those disobedient spirits had the truth preached to them is still further specified as "*while the ark was being prepared*" (κατασκευαζομένης κιβωτοῦ). It seems that the apostle is nervously anxious to show that the spirits in prison were those who lived just before the Flood. All the time during which the ark was being built, those wicked men had the opportunity of repenting of their sin and obtaining God's favour, and all that time did righteous Noah plead with them, so far as we know, in vain.

Ver. 20d. *Εἰς ἣν ὀλίγαι, τουτέστιν ὀκτώ, ψυχαὶ διεσώθησαν δι' ὕδατος*—"*Into which a few, that is, eight souls, were carried safely through water.*" Noah and his family, eight souls in all, were all, apparently, who availed themselves of the divine warning, and sought safety in the ark. All the rest perished in the waters of the Flood. They were saved from a watery grave. It was not the water that saved them. They were really saved *from* it. The version of 1611 says they were saved *by*, that of 1881 that they were saved *through*, water. The meaning is the same in both. Both represent water as the means of salvation. But, as every intelligent reader sees, it was the water of the Flood that was the source of danger. Noah and his family were saved *from* it; the others perished *by means of* it. The Revisers of 1881 are forced to put in the margin—"carried safely through water"; but they evidently hanker after the idea that the apostle meant that in some sense water here is to be regarded as securing salvation from death. The narrative in Genesis effectually disposes of such a notion.

But we must put the soul of the apostle's purpose into our exposition of vv. 19 and 20 to complete our work. The great leading peculiarity of these verses is that they describe Christ's anxiety to bring sinners to God. He is unwilling that any should perish. He waited long, and went personally to preach to the wicked men in Noah's time, and all to save eight souls. And let us exercise the same patience under suffering as He did under the opposition manifested to Him while on earth. O how precious is *a* soul! If by our example of patient submission to the divine will we can save one from perdition, we shall on that great day be greeted by the welcome, "Well done!"

## An Excursus on Ver. 21*a*

Ver. 21*a*. *Ὃ καὶ ὑμᾶς ἀντίτυπον νῦν σώζει*—"Which also is now saving you an antitype." Or, as we have translated above—"And this also is now saving you an antitype." The voluminous controversy which this and the following clause have occasioned has not led to a satisfactory settlement of its exegesis. We have never met with any explanation of the apostle's words here which we could accept. We propose an exposition which commends itself to our own mind, and which we humbly hope students of the New Testament will consider not unworthy of attention. We proceed upon the assumption which we have hitherto followed in these papers, that what an apostle has written was intended to be intelligible; and we argue that if there is confusion in our interpretation of his words, the fault must be ours, not his. If we hold less than this, how can we enter upon the study of his writings with any degree of confidence? This part of the passage which we have undertaken to expound is not, strictly speaking, connected with any question about *the spirits in prison*, but it is the conclusion of the sentence in which this expression occurs; and that sentence is not entirely occupied with this knotty subject. The great object of the apostle in the sentence, which is a long one, is to show how intense is Christ's desire to bring men to God. That desire is still dwelt upon in this clause.

Let us look for a little at a few of the interpretations of this clause which have been offered. And we need do little more than quote certain translations which have been given. These will indicate with sufficient accuracy for our purpose the views founded upon them.

It seems to have become very early a settled belief, that in this clause the apostle wished to compare baptism with something mentioned in the immediately preceding verse, and all interpreters have laboured since that time to make this comparison clear. No one hitherto appears to have been disposed to call in question the accuracy of this established belief. We hope to be able to prove that there is no comparison here made between baptism and anything mentioned in the preceding verse. This may seem a bold assertion, but we speak advisedly, and we hope the remaining portion of our paper will justify this boldness. But, meanwhile, let us make our proposed reference to published translations. The Vulgate rendering is, "*Quoad et vos nunc similis formæ salvos facit baptisma.*" This is simply unintelligible. Erasmus was justified, after quoting this version, in adding, "*Græca plus habent lucis.*" Zeger translates, "To which a similar baptism also now makes us safe." Not to mention other objections to this translation, it implies that a baptism of some kind or other has already been spoken of. But no one requires to be told that no such subject has been mentioned in the preceding context. Castalio's translation is intelligible, but is not a correct version of any Greek text extant: "*Consimili forma nunc quoque babtisma vos servat.*" Knatchbull reads the last two words of the preceding verse along with our text thus: "By water also baptism, which is the antitype (of the ark of Noah, wherein eight souls were saved), doth now save us." But this translation would imply that it had been said in the preceding verse that Noah and his family were saved *by water*. This would not be so, either in sound or sense, if you removed the expression in question from the preceding verse and prefixed it to the 21st. But, further, the words δι' ὕδατος, whatever meaning we assign to them, belong so evidently to διεσώθησαν, that it would be an act of violence to read them in any other connexion. But, once more, this translation makes baptism the antitype of the ark. Grammatically, this is impossible; but how can the resemblance between the two be made out logically? Dr. John Brown says, "The words may be rendered with perfect accuracy, which was a type or figure of the baptism which saves us." We cannot admit the accuracy of such a rendering. It is exposed to several serious objections. No Greek text ever heard of warrants such a translation. It arbitrarily alters the collocation of the apostle's words, as well as makes havoc of the rules of syntax. It reads baptism as in the genitive case, and calls in from the region of fancy another *which*, in order to complete a fictitious sense. If we are permitted to take such liberties as this with the word of God, we may make it teach anything we please. Alford's translation is as little intelligible as any we have yet mentioned: "Which, the antitype (of that) is now saving you also." If any of our readers can make sense out of this, or can construe it according to the rules of English syntax, all we can say is, that we envy them their ability. Our Revisers do not make the sense any plainer by the rendering: "Which also after a true likeness (*margin*, in the antitype), doth now save you." What is the comparison here? Is it in the fact of saving? Or is it between the water of the Flood and that of baptism? When we try to think out the meaning of our Revisers, we become involved in hopeless perplexity. We have shown at length that water in the preceding verse is viewed as an element of danger, not as securing salvation or preservation. Is it possible that correct expositions can be built upon such translations?

The question of textual criticism must be disposed of before we proceed further. What are the actual Greek words which we have to expound? What did Peter write? It is plain that we can make no satisfactory progress till this question is settled. A good deal of the diversity of translation exhibited in the preceding paragraph is due to variation of text. Did Peter write ὅ or ᾧ, and ὑμᾶς or ἡμᾶς? These are the alternative readings upon which we have to decide. There is a great preponderance of authority in favour of ὅ. No editor now ever dreams of accepting any other reading. There is more doubt whether we should read ὑμᾶς or ἡμᾶς. It is gratifying, however, to think that, whichever of these we accept, the meaning is not materially affected, nor is the grammatical construction interfered with. The three best codices, however,—the Sinaitic, the Vatican, and the Alexandrine, — read ὑμᾶς. We accept the text of Westcott and Hort. This is the text accepted by such men as Lachmann also, and Buttmann and Tischendorf. There is hardly any room for suspecting its perfect accuracy. We read, then, as follows, giving, however, for reasons which will afterwards appear, another than the ordinary punctuation: ὃ καὶ ὑμᾶς ἀντίτυπον νῦν σώζει. We regard this as the end of the sentence, and translate accordingly, "And this also is now saving you an antitype."

Our readers will observe that this translation is, in some respects, new. It is made to contain an assertion not hitherto ascribed to the apostle. Our rendering is, however, quite literal, and our only wonder is that it should never have been thought of before. We have been compelled to adopt the above punctuation, in order to make it possible to translate without violating the rules of Greek syntax. The construction of the clause is naturally completed with the word σώζει, and with that word the sentence must of necessity terminate. A new subject is introduced by the immediately succeeding word βάπτισμα. The hitherto received mode of punctuation used in this verse can lead to nothing but confusion, for it seeks to construe two distinct sentences with two distinct subjects, as if they were only one. We need hardly say that the punctuation of our Bibles is not of inspired authority. Every interpreter feels himself free to punctuate in such a way as he thinks will give the most natural, clear, and consistent sense to the words which he has to explain.

The first question raised in connexion with the *exposition* of the clause before us is, What is the antecedent to *which*? What is it that saves, according to the apostle's assertion? This question has received various answers, as our brief review of opinions has shown. Some say, *the ark*. But this is plainly inadmissible, either grammatically or logically. *Which* is neuter in Greek, and *ark* is feminine. Then how can the ark save *now*? The great body of interpreters answer the question now before us by saying, *water* is the antecedent. And they show great diligence in attempting to explain how *water* saves. It is not *water per se*, but *water* as used in baptism which secures this result— *Which water as the antitype baptism now saves you*, or, as the Revisers put it, *Which also, after a true likeness* (margin, *in the antitype*), *doth now save you*. Every one hitherto has assumed that baptism is here said to save. Those who believe in baptismal regeneration find this belief quite to their purpose. But many interpreters think the apostle no sooner wrote down this thought than he perceived it was too strong, and proceeded to qualify it by the language of the subsequent part of the verse. The plain English of this is, that the apostle made a clumsy job of it in attempting to say how baptism saves, and was compelled to make an explanation which involves the whole matter in hopeless confusion. This is certainly not very complimentary to Peter's command of Greek, not to mention his inspiration at all. But as this is the commonly received interpretation, we must subject it to a rigid scrutiny. It is exposed to several fatal objections. These objections we can state in answering the question, What is the antecedent to *which* ?

1. If we make *water* the antecedent, we require to establish a new doctrine of the relative. The hitherto received doctrine on this subject is, that the relative gathers up and repeats the idea of its antecedent. It includes nothing more and nothing less. It certainly does not include something totally different. But the view we are refuting overturns this doctrine. According to it, the relative and its antecedent represent two radically distinct thoughts. The water of the antecedent had destructive, the water of the relative has saving, properties. If the antecedent in

this case is water, then it is the water of the Flood which is meant, and it is the idea of this water which the relative ought to repeat. It is not any kind of water, but, specifically, the water of the Flood. So that the apostle's meaning must be—"which water of the Flood also now saves you." How such a doctrine accords with Scripture, we are not skilful enough to demonstrate. How could this water be obtained, even if we were persuaded of its saving efficacy? We are aware that those against whom we write do not understand the apostle's words thus; but we must have a new doctrine of the relative to read them in any other way, if we are to make water the antecedent.

2. If we make *water* the antecedent, we must go further, and make it synonymous with baptism. This is done by those against whom we write. But this is to confound things that differ. Water is used in Christian baptism; but water is not baptism. We might as well say that bread and wine are the Lord's Supper. We must not confound the elements used in the Christian sacraments with the sacraments themselves. We speak of a baptism of blood; but who would ever think of saying, baptism is blood? We read of the baptism of the Spirit; but who would ever think of saying that baptism is the Spirit? We read of a baptism of fire; but who would ever dream of saying, baptism is fire? Alford seems to have felt the force of this objection when he wrote: "Even baptism (not *the water* of baptism)—the parenthesis following is a kind of protest against such a rendering —but water, in the form of baptism, becomes to us baptism." Does this explanation make our readers any wiser? For our own part, it is a piece of logical

legerdemain, which we confess ourselves unable to follow. How does water, in the form of baptism, become to us baptism? When does water ever take the form of baptism? Alford's words are useful, however, as showing how vain is the attempt to identify water with baptism. In fact, the view which Alford adopts puts *which, antitype*, and *baptism* all in apposition, and makes them all synonymous with *water*. It is impossible to construe the first clause of the verse in any other way in accordance with the view which we condemn. Alford cannot escape from this impossibility by tagging on *baptism* to the end of the clause as a kind of appendix.

3. If we make *water* the antecedent, we confound the distinction between *type* and *antitype*, as these terms are used by theologians. Water, according to the ordinary view, is both type and antitype. Alford and others try to get over this confusion by saying that the water to which the relative refers is not the water of Noah's Flood, but water generally, the common term between type and antitype. This ingenious refinement, or desperate shift, as we ought rather to call it, has no warrant from the apostle's words. The water referred to by *which*, if water is the antecedent, is the water of Noah's Flood, and can be no other. The established laws of grammar are nothing, if this is not so. And if the water is the same in both cases, then type and antitype become identical.

4. If we make *water* the antecedent, we destroy the logical connexion of the apostle's words. This objection is the most overwhelming of all. It was urged long ago by Piscator. The water of the Flood, he pointed out, did not preserve anyone, but destroyed very many; but here mention is made of preservation.

## What led to Noah's Preservation

This objection is unanswerable. If you speak of the water of baptism as now saving, this implies that it has been spoken of before as saving. But every one knows that this is not the case. The water spoken of in the preceding verse drowned all the antediluvians excepting Noah and his family, who were preserved by special means. Entering the ark, they were *carried in safety through the water*,—διεσώθησαν δι᾽ ὕδατος,—which would otherwise have drowned them also. How, then, can water be said to save now *also*? But some try to escape from this objection by saying that it is baptism, as the antitype of the water of the Flood, which saves. Now, granting, for the sake of argument, that water and baptism are synonymous, does the explanation offered mend the matter much? The type and the antitype are not contrasts, but differ from one another only as the seal differs from the impression. They bear the very closest resemblance to one another. But how can there be any resemblance, as to effects at least,—and this is the matter to be attended to,—between the water of the Flood and the water of baptism? They point in opposite directions. The water of the Flood is associated with destruction, the water of baptism with salvation.

We hope we have taken our readers along with us up to this point, and that they agree with us in thinking that the antecedent to *which* cannot be *water*. The question of the antecedent may now be resolved into this other, What did Peter regard as leading to the preservation of Noah and his family? The answer which we obtain to this question will point out to us what is the antecedent to *which*. Our text expressly declares that what led to the salvation in the one case leads to salvation in the other. The apostle's words are, "which also now saves," etc., clearly showing that what saves now also preserved Noah and his family long ago. Now, what led to the preservation of Noah and his family?

Was it the preaching of Christ referred to in the 19th verse? There cannot be the slightest doubt that, but for the Redeemer's warning words to them, they would have shared in the general catastrophe. Steiger is forced to admit the influence which Christ's preaching had in securing the preservation of Noah and his family, though his view otherwise is far from sound. His words are: "What brought deliverance never was the water alone, but the word of God, which they believed, bringing them through the water." It is certainly in accordance with the narrative in Genesis to account for the deliverance of Noah and his family by the warning words which were received. At first sight it seems as if here we had found the answer which our question requires. But a moment's thought dissipates the illusion. The preaching of Christ to Noah and his contemporaries was preaching for those times, not for all ages. We cannot say that it is the warning which was addressed to the men of that time which saves us. The message then delivered was not the gospel, properly so called. Then, again, if you understand Peter to say that the preaching of Christ to Noah and his family led to their preservation, and if you thus make this preaching the antecedent to *which*, you destroy the structural unity of the sentence, which begins with the 18th verse and ends with the first clause of the 21st. Now, what is the leading idea in that sentence? A glance at it will show that its aim is to illustrate the operation of

Christ's desire to bring men to God. To say the very least, you obscure that aim if you ascribe the preservation of Noah and his family, and our salvation, to Christ's preaching to the antediluvians. The unity of thought in the sentence must be maintained. The apostle's thinking is clear, logical, and precise.

2. The true antecedent to *which*, is Christ's desire, as expressed in His preaching to the spirits in prison, and, especially, in His death and resurrection, to bring men to God. It was this which led Him to become our Substitute and die for us. It was this which led to the salvation of Noah and his family, and it is this which leads to our salvation now. This view maintains the structural unity of the sentence, and brings out a clear, consistent, and scriptural sense. This we shall endeavour to show as briefly as possible. In order to do this, we must first try to point out the purpose for which Peter wrote this sentence. Those whom the apostle addressed were exposed, it appears, to very considerable trials. These trials, the apostle reminds them, were sent upon them in accordance with the divine will. They were appointed to them for a good and wise purpose, and if they would submit to them, much benefit would accrue to the cause of religion. The sufferings of the saints, promote God's glory—" the blood of the martyrs is the seed of the Church." Let them be animated with the desire to bring men to God, even though, in carrying out that desire, they might be called upon to suffer even to death. To enforce his appeal, the apostle introduces the example of Christ, and shows how He, in carrying out His desire to bring men to God, died on the cross, preached to the antediluvians, and now saves His people. Peter's sentence contains three main mem-

bers, each of which exhibits an illustration of Christ's desire to bring men to God. And these members stand to one another in the closest logical relation. Christ died to bring men to God; in pursuance of which object or desire He even—$\hat{\epsilon}\nu\ \hat{\omega}\ \kappa\alpha\acute{\iota}$—preached to the antediluvians of Noah's day; which object, or desire, or purpose, also—$\hat{o}\ \kappa\alpha\acute{\iota}$—now saves men. Is it because this construction is so simple that it has hitherto evaded the notice of interpreters?

We do not require any elaboration of argument to prove that the salvation of men is due to Christ's desire to bring them to God. This desire has been at the foundation of all the gracious arrangements which have been made for the good of our race. This desire our Saviour is carrying out in connexion with the special appliances of the gospel. These appliances are all saturated with His intense love to our souls. So that we can say, it is the Lord who adds daily to the Church such as shall be saved.

The use of the word *antitype* by the apostle shows that the preservation of Noah and his family in the ark is to be regarded as typical of the salvation of sinners from the wrath to come. One of the great fundamental principles of the relation between the type and the antitype is, that the series of ideas connected with the latter occupies, as it were, a higher platform than that occupied by the former. Thus Abraham and David were types, Christ is the antitype. And while all the points in which these Old Testament saints resemble Christ are found in them in an imperfect form, in Him they are found in perfection. This principle is illustrated in the present case. The mere statement of the points of resemblance is all that is necessary to show this. In the case of Noah and his family, the blessing secured was bodily preservation; in the case of those saved through the appliances of the gospel, it is the eternal well-being of the soul;—in the case of Noah and his family, the preaching to which they listened was connected with the coming Flood; in the case of those whose souls are saved now, it is the message of the gospel;—in the case of Noah and his family, the preaching was adapted to that age only; in the case of those who hear now, it is adapted to all who live under the New Testament dispensation;—in the case of Noah and his family, only eight persons were saved from destruction; the ransomed of the gospel dispensation constitute a multitude which no man can number.

We construe the word *antitype* as in apposition with the pronoun *you*. Are we justified in doing so? Our right can hardly be disputed. All grammarians admit that the appositive word naturally, and very generally, follows the main noun or pronoun. But it may be said, How can *you* and *antitype* be in apposition, for the one word is singular and the other plural? Here we must apologise for being elementary, but our excuse is that we are anxious to carry every one of our readers along with us. It is a well-known rule in grammar, that while words in apposition must be in the same case, they need not be of the same number. Ἀντίτυπον may be either in the nominative or accusative case, so far as its form is concerned; but it makes confusion, as we have already shown, to read it as a nominative, and construe it in apposition with *which*. The construction which we follow is easy and natural. The following examples of plurals and singulars in apposition are given by Winer: "Therefore, my *brethren*, dearly beloved and longed for, my *joy* and my *crown.*" " And hath made *us* a *kingdom* "—the true reading of Rev. i. 6. We are pleased to have the support of Dr. Hort here. He says, Westcott and Hort's *Greek Testament,* vol. ii. Appendix, p. 102: "The order of the words renders it impossible to take ἀντίτυπον with βάπτισμα, whether in apposition to ὅ or to the sentence, as though it were either ἀντίτυπον ὄν or ἀντιτύπως." So far we are glad to agree with so distinguished a scholar, but we must protest in the most strenuous manner against what follows: "Accordingly, ὅ seems to be a primitive error for ᾧ, the force of which may be hidden by the interposition of καὶ ὑμᾶς before ἀντίτυπον; this deviation from the more obvious order is justified by the emphasis on καὶ ὑμᾶς." This is conjectural emendation with a vengeance! Where will such a mode of criticism land us? The MSS. are quite decisive against Dr. Hort's suggestion. And the reading which he suggests is exposed to the mass of objections which we have stated above.

We have not ventured to express any opinion as to the eternal state of those who perished in the Flood, or as to the way in which those who have never had the opportunity of hearing the gospel, or whose opportunity has been insufficient from one cause or another, will be judged. To have done so would have been, in our opinion, an impious interference in a matter which God has not been pleased to reveal. We are quite satisfied to leave the judgment of all men in God's hands. "Shall not the Judge of all the earth do right?" We dare not speak of the possibility of a state of probation in another world. The passages we have quoted in our exposition of clause 19*a* forbid, we believe, the entertainment of such a thought. We regard much of what has been written about the so-called Wider Hope as neither fitted to promote God's glory nor to advance the interests of religion. Surely we may leave it to the mercy of God to dispense to the heathen, and to those who have never been in a position to receive the gospel, the benefits of Christ's atoning sacrifice, if He thinks proper. We have no right to pronounce dogmatically one way or other. We think the feeling of true devoutness is to say, all this matter is safe in the hands of a just and righteous God.

# IV

# THE SIGNIFICANCE OF BAPTISM IN RELATION TO OUR SALVATION

### An Exegetical Study

Βάπτισμα οὐ σαρκὸς ἀπόθεσις ῥύπου ἀλλὰ συνειδήσεως ἀγαθῆς ἐπερώτημα εἰς Θεὸν δι' ἀναστάσεως Ἰησοῦ Χριστοῦ, ὅς ἐστιν ἐν δεξιᾷ τοῦ Θεοῦ, πορευθεὶς εἰς οὐρανόν, ὑποταγέντων αὐτῷ ἀγγέλων καὶ ἐξουσιῶν καὶ δυνάμεων.

"Baptism is not a putting away of the filth of the flesh, but the request of a good conscience towards God, through the resurrection of Jesus Christ: who is on the right hand of God, having gone into heaven; angels, and authorities, and powers, being made subject unto him."—1 Pet. iii. 21b–22.

In the preceding paper we have shown the impossibility of construing βάπτισμα along with ἀντίτυπον in the first clause of ver. 21. The collocation of words, as well as the confusion and unintelligibility of thought thereby produced, forbids such a construction. The clause reaches its natural termination with the verb σώζει. The question is one quite as much of grammar and punctuation as of exegesis. And, of course, no one claims infallibility for the punctuation in either the Greek or the English New Testament. Every scholar has the right to accept the punctuation which brings out the best and most consistent sense.

One wonders why a simple glance at the order of the words has not been considered sufficient to settle the matter long ago. There they are: "Ὅ καὶ ὑμᾶς ἀντίτυπον νῦν σώζει. That is, "Which you an antitype now saves." Or, in more elegant and correct English, "And this also is now saving you an antitype. Is that not sufficiently intelligible? We have shown in our preceding paper that that brings out a good and consistent sense, and in harmony with the foregoing context. Those to whom the apostle wrote were an antitype or copy of those saved in the ark from the destructive waters of the Flood. And these, again, were saved because of Christ's desire to bring men to God.

Our belief is that if the clause had not received a twist from some interpreter in early Christian times, no one would have dreamt of construing it otherwise than as we do. And we further think that if Sacramentarian ideas had not blinded the minds of modern expositors, the traditional construction would long ere this have been abandoned. The meaning of the clause when βάπτισμα is read along with it is involved in hopeless confusion. To read it so is forced and unnatural. This may not be admitted in so many words, but there is abundant evidence of the fact in the interpretations which have been attempted. In these interpretations, as Dr. Hort shows, the rules of Greek syntax are violently set aside. We may add that they also outrage common sense. To force βάπτισμα into the construction is like attempting to mix oil and water together. But the worst of it all is that, when this violence is used, though the clause is thereby made, to careful thought, ungrammatical and unintelligible, yet, to superficial examination, it seems to teach, on the subject of baptism, a doctrine nowhere else found in Scripture.

Of course, there are always the ignorance and literary deficiency of the apostle to fall back upon, if any one complains that the clause, as usually construed, is unintelligible. He was so little able, poor man, to write intelligible Greek that he made sad blunders in his efforts to express himself. It is a pity his interpreters have been born so late. Had they lived in his day, they would have put him right. For, of course, they have no doubt that Peter wished to say that there is a saving efficacy in baptism. And *their* wisdom finds in his words what *he* failed clearly to express. But seriously, we humbly think that our apostle was quite as well able to convey his meaning as his learned critics. And we are sure he would repudiate their method of construing his words in this clause of which we have been speaking.

Grammarians are here the primary offenders. The division of our Bibles into verses has helped to perpetuate their offence. How easy would the work of the exegete have been, if a period had been put after σώζει! By correcting the punctuation, we have been able to give a new turn to the apostle's words, and to bring them into harmony with what is said in Scripture elsewhere. And to make the matter more emphatic, we have resolved to take a new paper to discuss this second clause and those others that remain in this and the following verse.

This clause stands in the Greek without any verb. In such a case the simple expedient is to supply ἐστί after βάπτισμα. The substantive verb is often omitted by Greek writers in propositions, and must, of course, be applied when translating into English, for the genius of our language is different from that of Greek. No scholar will say that we use any violence in supplying the substantive verb here. We go further, and say that they must admit that the sense requires it. The words, "not the putting away of the filth of the flesh," are admittedly used with regard to baptism. They are, in fact, the predicate of a sentence in which the subject is *baptism*. And the scholarly expedient is to connect the subject and predicate with the copula ἐστί.

But let us, for the sake of argument, admit that βάπτισμα may be construed as part of the preceding clause. How does this affect the sense of this clause now before us? It becomes decapitated. It contradicts, besides, the preceding clause. That clause, with βάπτισμα taken into it, says that baptism saves; the clause now before us, that it does *not* put away the filth of the flesh, that is, *does not save*. A more complete contradiction could hardly be conceived. It is of the very essence of salvation that it puts away the filth of the flesh—the corruption of our fallen nature. This corruption constitutes the danger of our fallen state. If we are not delivered from this danger we perish. How the Sacramentarians can escape from this dilemma we cannot tell. We are thankful that we run no danger of being impaled by it. And observe, we do not make this difficulty; it is made by those whom we are seeking to refute. Can any believer in inspiration suppose that Peter is the author of this absurdity? And if this absurdity does not logically arise out of the construction to which we object, all we can say is, then language must have been invented to confound thought! We do not expect to be thanked in certain quarters for these criticisms, but truth is more precious to us than any man's approval.

But perhaps some one may say we are putting too strict a meaning upon the word saves—σώζει. To meet this objection it is enough to point out that the verb to *save* and its cognate *salvation* always presuppose the idea of danger, either physical or spiritual. They are used in connexion with disease. When our Lord is represented as healing a diseased person, the individual is said to be *saved*. When the words are used in connexion with the soul, the danger of perdition is presupposed. The verb and its cognate are never used in the Bible in the sense which Sacramentarians assign to them. Nor are they ever used there as synonymous with conversion, as in the current theology of the present day. It would be simply a waste of time to prove this.

But before attempting anything like a formal exposition of the words before us, we must face the question, Why does Peter introduce the subject of baptism at all? If this ordinance was not suggested to his mind by the water of the Flood, how do we account for the apostle's mention of it? It is admitted on all hands that the apostle had in his mind's eye a misconception regarding this sacrament which he wished to remove. This misconception is sufficient to account for his reference to this Christian rite. There is a constant tendency in the human mind to rest in outward forms. There is a large ritualistic element in all our natures, and this element is constantly cropping out and assuming more or less magnitude. We know that very early baptism was regarded as of the nature of an *opus operatum*. This belief actually led some to delay this ordinance till the hour of death, so that as they passed from life they might be cleansed by the magical annihilation of their sins, and, without hindrance, enter into glory. The words of the apostle here lead us to infer that this heresy had already begun to take shape in the Church. Peter therefore strikes at its root in the incisive words of this second clause of ver. 21. He contemplates a reader as saying: "I have been baptized. Do I require anything else in order to salvation? Does not this cleanse me from all sin, and secure for me a place in heaven? Has not all been done that is essential to my salvation, when I have submitted to this Christian rite?" And the apostle, in effect, replies: "No; you have formed quite a false idea as to the relation in which baptism stands to salvation. Baptism is merely the expression of your desire to be saved, but this desire cannot take you to heaven apart from lifelong and constant application to Christ. The apostle was thus led to explain what baptism is, in relation to our salvation. He does not give us a definition, properly so called, of this rite. He merely gives us such an account of it as is necessary to refute the false idea regarding it already referred to. His teaching takes first a negative, and then a positive form.

1. He tells us what baptism is not, in relation to our salvation. It is "not, a putting away of the filth of the flesh." The common explanation of the word *flesh* here is the outward part of our bodies—the skin. Of course, the matter is not put in so pointed a form as that, but such is the thought. And the idea is, that the apostle wishes to say that baptism does not cleanse away the outward impurities of the body. Steiger says, "The full sense is, not the

laying aside of bodily filth, consequently the laying aside of what is spiritual." And he quotes Justin Martyr, *Dialog. con. Tryph.*: "For what is the benefit of that baptism (the Jewish lustration) which cleanses the flesh and the body only?" Now, on what conceivable grounds can we suppose the apostle would make such a statement, if that be the meaning of his words? Who ever held that baptism is mere washing? Whether the ordinance be administered by the immersion of the whole body, or by the sprinkling of a portion of it, the result is not to wash the skin. Wetting is not washing. Surely the apostle had something more important on hand than to refute so frivolous an idea as that with which his commentators have credited him. Besides, is there any instance in the New Testament where *flesh* is used in the sense of skin? Evidently, the word *flesh* here has the same meaning as we have assigned to it in the 18th verse—man's corrupt nature; and the intention of the apostle is to say that the mere rite of baptism cannot remove the corruption of our fallen nature. The removal of this requires a much more powerful agency than the observance of any mere rite.

2. The apostle next states what is the actual relation in which baptism stands to our salvation. It is "not, a putting away of the filth of the flesh, but the request of a good conscience toward God," etc. The main difficulty here is to determine the meaning of the word which we have translated *request*—ἐπερώτημα. Our Authorised Version translates *answer*. The Revision of 1881 gives us in the body of the text the rendering, *interrogation*, and in the margin the alternatives, *inquiry* or *appeal*. And many infer that *answer* must be the meaning of the term, because

they imagine there is here an allusion to the answers given to the questions put to candidates for baptism in early Christian times. Grotius says, regarding these questions, "In baptism the bishop, or some other in his name, in this manner inquired, or, which is the same thing, stipulated, Do you renounce Satan? The person about to be baptized said, I renounce him. Again he was asked, Do you adhere to Christ? He replied, I do adhere to Him." This, Tertullian, in his treatise on baptism, calls "the engagement of salvation." He also says, in his treatise on the resurrection of the flesh, "The soul is sanctified, not by the washing, but by the response." There is no evidence, however, that such questions as these were put to those who received baptism in Peter's time. Besides, the proper meaning of ἐπερώτημα is not *answer*, but *request*, or at least something which looks for an answer. It is derived from the verb ἐπερωτάω, I ask. Bengel makes it mean *interrogatio*, or *rogatio*, *question*. And undoubtedly the word sometimes bears this meaning. Wiesinger makes it *prayer* or *desire*. Alford, while not thinking himself perfectly correct, translates *inquiry*. Wiesinger seems to us to give the true sense. A prayer is not an inquiry. But how is baptism a request or prayer? It is only, of course, constructively such. The man who seeks baptism reveals the same state of mind as that exemplified by the man who prays. He expresses, in no ambiguous manner, his belief in the purifying doctrines of the gospel, and his desire to secure the benefits which the gospel offers. Baptism is the ordinance which has been appointed for marking our connexion with the religion of Jesus. That religion is associated with many benefits. By baptism, therefore, we make application for the bestowal of these benefits. We do our part in connexion with the covenant made with men in Christ, and we show our determination to look to our Redeemer for what is necessary for our salvation.

What, then, are we to regard as the request which baptism presents? The answer to this question is to be gathered from the antithesis between the second and third clauses of ver. 21, "Baptism is not a putting away of the filth of the flesh, but the request of a good conscience toward God," etc. The clear inference from these words is, that what cannot be secured through the mere rite of baptism, is secured through the request of a good conscience. It is by divine agency alone that moral pollution can be removed. Christianity is a purifying system. By being baptized, and thus embracing that divine system, we put ourselves in Christ's hands for the purification of our natures. We ask Him to do for us what He has engaged to do. It is the disposition, therefore, which we bring to the baptismal font, and not the mere outward observance, which we are to look to. But, supposing the disposition at the time of baptism were everything that could be desired, is that efficacious for our perfect sanctification? No one who knows anything about the teaching of Scripture will embrace such an opinion. The believer's sanctification is a gradual thing; and, in order to our being made perfect in holiness, we must, throughout life, strive to maintain a good conscience by cleaving to Christ, looking to Him for His grace, and seeking to live up to our light. The request which is presented in baptism will lead to the putting away of the filth of the flesh, but only if it is a lifelong desire. The removal of all moral impurity is synchronous with our salvation. So that we may express the spirit of the prayer which baptism presents as a desire to be brought to God, or a wish to be saved, or a desire to be sanctified wholly. Hence we cannot agree with Alford, who makes it the prayer for a good conscience, which, he says, is the aim and end of the Christian baptismal life. The form of words used by Peter refutes such an opinion. Baptism is "the request of a good conscience." The good conscience is there, and the request is its outcome. The good conscience precedes, does not succeed, baptism.

But what is the exact meaning to be attached to the words, *a good conscience toward God*? There can be no question that the thought which they express is one and indivisible. Paul, in Acts xxiii. 1, is represented as expressing a similar thought, "Brethren, I have lived before God in all good conscience until this day." In the same Book of Acts, xxiv. 16, he is represented as saying, "Herein do I also exercise myself to have a conscience void of offence toward God and men alway." The grammatical form in both of these passages is different from that in our text, but we are not here raising any question of grammar. The exact thought is what we wish to get at. A *good conscience*, or one *void of offence toward God*, is evidently one which cannot blame itself for disobedience to God. It is one enlightened by divine truth and loyal to God's will. Its possessor has turned from the ways of sin, and has resolved to obey God according to his lights. His heart is in the divine service. And, as baptism is an ordinance instituted by Christ, he feels that he must observe it. In the preceding context we read of Christ's desire to bring men to God, and of the remarkable means which He once adopted to gratify that desire. When a man submits himself to baptism, or brings his child to receive the ordinance, he thereby responds to this desire on the part of Christ. He shows that he is ready to accept the benefits which Christ died to secure for mankind. The preceding context expresses what Christ has done for man's salvation, here there is expressed what man himself has to do. The two things are the counterparts of one another. We cannot obtain the benefits of Christ's death unless we make application for them. In short, submission to baptism is the act of a believer.

But to whom are we to regard the prayer in baptism as addressed? The answer to this question must be, *to Christ*. He has, in His bestowal, all that a man needs to bring him to God. He can enlighten him by His Spirit, and guide him into all truth. And He can give him all the help required to enable him to overcome all the difficulties of the divine life, and triumph over all his spiritual foes. Baptism is often spoken of as *into the name of Christ*, that is, as expressive of faith in Him. In Acts viii. 16 we are told that the Holy Ghost had not as yet fallen upon any of the Samaritan converts, "only they had been baptized into the name of the Lord Jesus." When Paul came to Ephesus (Acts xix.) he found certain disciples there. They had not received the Holy Ghost, and had heard only of John's baptism. Paul said to them (vv. 4, 5), "John baptized with the baptism of repentance, saying unto the people that they should believe on Him which should come after him, that is, on Jesus. And when they heard this, they were baptized into the name of the Lord Jesus." So also in Rom. vi. 3 and Gal. iii. 27. It requires no argument to show that the idea underlying these passages is that submission to baptism implies faith in Christ, and the desire to look to Him for all the grace which the divine life requires.

This interpretation is confirmed by Acts xxii. 16, "Arise, and have yourself baptized, and your sins washed away, calling on His name." To understand these words, we must bear in mind the well-known grammatical principle, that when two imperatives are connected by καί, the first sometimes contains the condition under which the action indicated by the second will take place. The application of this principle leads us to say that Paul was here exhorted to have himself baptized, in order that his sins might be washed away, which is exactly the sentiment uttered by Peter on the day of Pentecost: "Repent ye, and be baptized, every one of you, in the name of Jesus Christ, unto the remission of sins"—εἰς ἄφεσιν ἁμαρτιῶν (Acts ii. 38). The expression, "calling on His name," is expository of what goes before. When Paul submitted to baptism in order to have his sins washed away, he was then and thereby calling on the name of Christ. He was presenting a prayer in acted form.

According to the view which we take of the apostle's words, a very good sense might have been brought out of them if we had accepted the rendering of ἐπερώτημα given in the Authorised Version, *answer*. Baptism would then be regarded as the *answer* or *response* to Christ's desire to bring men to God. But we believe that, on the whole, the rendering, *request*, is to be preferred, especially in view of the words of Acts xxii. 16.

The believer is encouraged to present his appeal to Christ through His resurrection. By that event he is assured that Christ is able to do all that He has undertaken to do. Christ's rising from the dead is the greatest of all arguments for faith in Him. We are justified in looking to Him as the channel through which comes all that is essential to our sanctification and salvation. God has committed the whole work of our salvation to His hands. And Christ has done everything necessary to qualify Him for His exalted office. He has fully met all the claims of justice, and has taken every barrier out of the way of our being reconciled to God. And God has raised Him from the dead in token of His satisfaction with the work which He had given Him to do.

The believer is still further encouraged to look to Christ by the assurance that He is *on the right hand of God*. This is not only a position of the highest honour, it is also one of the greatest authority. It implies that He is made the governor of the universe. It takes for granted the truth of the words which He spoke to His disciples just before His ascension: "All authority hath been given unto Me in heaven and on earth" (Matt. xxviii. 18). He sits on His mediatorial throne, still seeking, in His government, to carry forward the work which He did on earth, in order to bring men to God. This throne He will occupy till He hath put all enemies under His feet.

The dependent clause, *having gone into heaven*, seems to come in a little awkwardly. It places Christ's ascension into heaven after His session at the Father's right hand. This, of course, is not the natural order. What can be our apostle's reason for adopting this order? The only explanation which presents itself to our mind is that thereby an ambiguity is avoided. The Authorised Version translates this and the preceding clause thus: "Who is gone into heaven, and is on the right hand of God." This order, if it had been adopted by the apostle, might have conveyed the idea that Peter wished to say that *the angels, authorities, and powers*, spoken of in the clause which follows, are subject to the Father. But the apostle's wish was to bring prominently out the thought that these are subject to Christ as mediatorial governor of the universe, and that they are at His command for the benefit of believers.

The last clause of the passage before us, "*angels, and authorities, and powers, being made subject unto Him,*" we regard as similar in meaning to the words of Paul in Phil. ii. 10. "That in the name of Jesus every knee should bow, of those in heaven, of those on earth, and of those under the earth." All intelligent beings in God's universe are put under Christ's authority, both those who are loyal to God and those who are in rebellion against Him. The *angels* we take as the unfallen servants of heaven—those who have kept their first estate. These are at the command of Christ for the good of His people. "Are they not" (that is, the angels) "all ministering spirits, sent forth to do service for the sake of them that shall inherit salvation?" *The authorities and powers* we take to mean the evil spirits who seek to bring believers into subjection to the great enemy of mankind. Christ has power over them, and can protect His people from their malign influence. It is evident, therefore, that all that the apostle has written in the words which we have been considering in this paper were intended to show what encouragement a believer has to submit to baptism, and thereby to profess his confidence in Christ as his Saviour, and his conviction that Christ is able and willing to give him all that he needs to bring him to God and to glory.

# V

# BELIEVERS DEAD TO SIN, BUT RAISED TO LIFE WITH CHRIST

## An Exegetical Study [1]

Καὶ ὑμᾶς ὄντας νεκροὺς τοῖς παραπτώμασι καὶ ταῖς ἁμαρτίαις ὑμῶν, ἐν αἷς ποτὲ περιεπατήσατε κατὰ τὸν αἰῶνα τοῦ κόσμου τούτου, κατὰ τὸν ἄρχοντα τῆς ἐξουσίας τοῦ ἀέρος, τοῦ πνεύματος τοῦ νῦν ἐνεργοῦντος ἐν τοῖς υἱοῖς τῆς ἀπειθείας ἐν οἷς καὶ ἡμεῖς πάντες ἀνεστράφημέν ποτε ἐν ταῖς ἐπιθυμίαις, τῆς σαρκὸς ἡμῶν, ποιοῦντες τὰ θελήματα τῆς σαρκὸς καὶ τῶν διανοιῶν, καὶ ἤμεθα τέκνα φύσει ὀργῆς, ὡς καὶ οἱ λοιποί·—ὁ δὲ Θεὸς, πλούσιος ὢν ἐν ἐλέει, διὰ τὴν πολλὴν ἀγάπην αὐτοῦ ἣν ἠγάπησεν ἡμᾶς, καὶ ὄντας ἡμᾶς νεκροὺς τοῖς παραπτώμασι συνεζωοποίησε τῷ Χριστῷ (χάριτί ἐστε σεσωσμένοι), καὶ συνήγειρε, καὶ συνεκάθισεν ἐν τοῖς ἐπουρανοις ἐν Χριστῷ Ἰησοῦ· ἵνα ἐνδείξηται ἐν τοῖς αἰῶσι τοῖς ἐπερχομένοις τὸ ὑπερβάλλον πλοῦτος τῆς χάριτος αὐτοῦ ἐν χρηστότητι ἐφ' ἡμᾶς ἐν Χριστῷ Ἰησοῦ.

"You also who are dead to your trespasses and sins; wherein aforetime ye walked according to the course of this world, according to the prince of the power of the air, of the spirit that now worketh in the sons of disobedience : among whom we also all once lived in the lusts of our flesh, doing the desires of the flesh and of the mind ; and were by nature children of wrath, even as the rest—God, I say, who is rich in mercy, for His great love wherewith He loved us, did us also, who are dead to our trespasses, quicken together with Christ (by grace have ye been saved), raise up together, and make sit together among the most exalted in Christ Jesus, that in the ages to come He might show the exceeding riches of His grace, in His kindness toward us, in Christ Jesus."—Revised Version (revised).—Eph. ii. 1-7.

THE writer of this paper believes that the Revisers of 1881 have, in common with their predecessors of 1611, failed to exhibit a perfectly accurate representation of the apostle's meaning in this part of his

[1] Reprinted from the *Homiletic Review*, 1893.

Epistle. This belief induces him to attempt to put before his readers what he thinks Paul actually wished to say. His exposition, if found to be satisfactory, must be his apology for differing from a body of men so learned and eminent as the Revisers. If his exposition prove unsatisfactory, he is aware that he exposes himself to the charge of presumption. He puts forward his views with some confidence, but not, he trusts, without due modesty. He accepts the Greek text adopted by the Revisers.

The first thing necessary is to indicate in a few words the connexion between the words under consideration and the preceding chapter. In the first chapter the apostle speaks of "the strength of God's might which He wrought in Christ when He raised Him from the dead, and made Him to sit at His right hand among the most exalted," etc. In the words before us, he points out the parallel between what God has done for Christ and what He has done for his readers, himself, and all believers.

Were our Revisers justified in inserting in the 1st verse the words *did He quicken*? This appears to be not only unnecessary, but tends to obscure the construction of the apostle's words and confuse the sense. The expression is borrowed ostensibly from the 5th verse, and is intended, apparently, to represent the meaning of συνεζωοποίησε. This verb, as all allow, governs ὑμᾶς. But so also do συνήγειρε and συνεκάθισεν. Why should the one verb be brought into the 1st verse to eke out the construction, and not the others? The course adopted by the Revisers in this matter, therefore, seems unwarrantable. They dislocate the apostle's words for a purpose which our translation shows to be wholly unnecessary. They follow the example of the Revisers of 1611; but that is no justification. It seems, too, a most unscholarly and extraordinary thing to borrow an explanatory phrase from a verse so far forward. Had they acted in a precisely opposite way, and borrowed from a verse as far away back, we could have better understood their conduct. This would have been intelligible. But, further, why do they use the emphatic form *did quicken* in the 1st verse and the ordinary form *quickened* in the 5th verse? There can surely be no warrant for this variation, except some supposed necessity which does not appear on the surface. But a still stronger objection to the course which the Revisers have adopted remains to be stated. Not only should they have brought up all the three verbs which govern ὑμᾶς, if they thought it necessary to bring up any at all, but they ought to have added the words *together with Christ*. The sense of the apostle requires this addition. The words *did quicken*, besides, do not express the full meaning of συνεζωοποίησε. The συν- is left without any English equivalent. How such an oversight should have occurred passes comprehension!

Our main objection to the Revisers' version of this passage is to the rendering of the words ὄντας νεκροὺς τοῖς παραπτώμασι καὶ ταῖς ἁμαρτίαις. These words they translate as if the particle ἐν occurred before τοῖς παραπτώμασι. And, in common with the Revisers of 1611, they regard the clause as a description of men in their unconverted state. This view, we may say, is universally adopted. To assail it seems like an attempt to lead a forlorn hope. The Revisers of 1881 make a very slight modification of the rendering of their predecessors of 1611. Instead of *dead in*, they translate *dead through*; but this change does not materially affect the sense. And both sets of Revisers take ὄντας as an imperfect. The participle ὤν seldom occurs in this sense, and therefore there is a strong presumption against its being so translated in this case. There are, we think, unanswerable objections against the clause in question being taken as a description of unconverted men and translated as the Revisers have done. 1. This view makes dead men walk. "When ye were dead through your trespasses and sins, wherein aforetime ye walked." It is not enough to say that this is a paradox. We have no right to ascribe to any writer an inconsistent idea like this without necessity. Our translation shows that there is no such necessity. The idea is grotesque and inconceivable, and ought not to be ascribed to the clear-minded Paul. We say with confidence, such an idea is not warranted here, nor in any other part of the New Testament. *Walking in sin* and *living in sin* are Pauline ideas as applicable to unconverted men, but not *dead in sin* or *through sin*. The apostle is not here so much writing rhetorically as giving a description in what, with him, are technical terms. To what spiritual condition his description applies we shall see by and by, but it cannot be to that of unconverted men. 2. This view destroys man's responsibility. A dead man is incapable of either thought or action. Extreme Calvinism makes men entirely passive in conversion, and some take pleasure in quoting this passage in support of such a position; but the whole teaching of the New Testament is opposed to such an idea. The whole Bible appeals to our reason and conscience, and tells us that our condemnation or salvation will turn entirely upon our rejection or reception of the truth.

If men are dead *in* sins, or *through* sins, they are, *ipso facto*, incapable of obeying the gospel, and are no longer accountable beings. According to the view which the Revisers take of the clause, the words mean totally subjected to sin, as a corpse is to the power of death, and as incapable of rising from it as that is of being restored to life. The Christian intelligence of the present day will not accept such a view. 3. The expression " dead in " or " through transgressions and sins " would, properly, apply, not to unconverted men, but to souls condemned to perdition. As reported in John viii. 21, our Lord said to the Jews on one occasion, " I go away, and ye shall seek Me, and shall die in your sin"—καὶ ἐν τῇ ἁμαρτίᾳ ὑμῶν ἀποθανεῖσθε. Should anyone try to escape from the application of this passage to the case in hand by saying that ἁμαρτίᾳ is in the singular, whereas in the passage before us the plural is used, we have to observe that, in the 24th verse of the same chapter, the words occur in the plural, as if the Lord, foreseeing the possibility of such an objection, wished to obviate it : " I said, therefore, unto you, that ye shall die in your sins ; for except ye believe that I am He, ye shall die in your sins "—ἀποθανεῖσθε ἐν ταῖς ἁμαρτίαις ὑμῶν. Now, observe that these Jews whom our Lord was addressing were unconverted men. They refused to believe that He was the great promised Messiah. They were in their sins—*living in them, walking in them*, but not *dead* in or *through* them. They would not be in that state till they had died in unbelief. It is plain, therefore, that our Lord's words are not in harmony with the view which the Revisers have adopted. Our Lord teaches us to regard the expression *dead in* or *through sins* as applicable only to souls condemned to perdition. It does not need to be said that no one understands the apostle, in the passage under consideration, to be referring to men in that state. He classes himself with those whom he describes; and he was a believer, rejoicing in the consciousness that his sins were pardoned.

But to this argument, founded upon our Lord's words, it may be objected that perhaps our Lord and Paul use the same words in different senses—that is to say, while our Lord might use the words which we have quoted from John's Gospel as applicable to souls condemned to perdition, our apostle might use them in the sense adopted by the Revisers. To show that this is not so, let us take a passage in which Paul uses the preposition ἐν—1 Cor. xv. 17, "If Christ hath not been raised, your faith is vain; ye are yet in your sins"— ἐν ταῖς ἁμαρτίαις ὑμῶν. "Then they also which have fallen asleep in Christ have perished"—ἀπώλοντο. Here the idea is precisely the same as our Lord's. Pardon is dependent upon the truth of the gospel. That, again, is dependent upon the resurrection of Christ. If the resurrection of Christ be not a fact, then no one of those to whom Paul was writing was pardoned. They were still in their sins; and those who had died, believing the gospel to be true, had died in their sins—that is, unforgiven, and exposed to the wrath of God. They were souls eternally condemned—νεκροὶ ἐν ταῖς ἁμαρτίαις. The word ἀπώλοντο is even stronger than νεκροί; but undoubtedly it applies to the state of souls consigned to perdition. Since, therefore, the words under consideration cannot apply to unconverted men, and since it is impossible to take them as referring to souls eternally condemned, there seems no alternative but to translate them as we have done—"who are dead to your trespasses and sins."[1]

Being constrained, for the reasons we have given, to translate ver. 1 as we have done, for the same reasons we are compelled to take that verse as Paul's technical description of one side of the believer's life. All who have undergone the great spiritual change are *dead to sin*, and *alive to God* and to *righteousness*. This is a form of phraseology in which Paul delights. He does not mean by it that the believer does not sin. He speaks theoretically, ideally. He means that the believer ought to have as little to do with sin as a dead man has with the affairs of life. He speaks in the same way of being *dead to the law*, and *dead from the rudiments of the world*. This death in Paul's mind is logically and theoretically bound up in the death of Christ. He says (2 Tim. ii. 11), " If we died with Him "; and in Col. iii. 3, " Ye died, and your life is hid with Christ in God." And as the death referred to is bound up in Christ's death, so are all the active graces and privileges of the Christian bound up in the life and honour now enjoyed by Christ in glory. Hence all the verbs in this passage referring to the Christian's posi-

---

[1] Estius, a Roman Catholic theologian of great learning and exegetical genius (born at Grocum in Holland 1542, died 1613), seems to have been the first to suggest this translation. His words, as given in *Poole's Synopsis, in loco*, are: "Phrasis hic accipi possit, ut Rom. vi. 2, 11, q.d. Et vos qui jam estis mortui peccatis vestris, i.e. non amplius in iis viventes, nihil qui commercii cum iis amplius habentes, *convivificavit Christo*, etc., ut infra, v. 5. Significatur autem ordo naturæ inter hæc duo, peccato mortuum esse, et Christo convivificari. Estque allusio ad baptismi ceremoniam, in qua prius est immergi, id est, mysticè, mori peccato, posterius emergere, i.e. ad vitam justitiæ exsurgere. Sensus hic probabilis est, tamen non facilè recedendum à communi expositione." No one hitherto, so far as we have been able to discover, has followed up the opinion here expressed. The *communis expositio* has up till now been accepted as indisputable.

tion are compounded with συν-, and have their meaning completed by the explanatory words τῷ Χριστῷ.

The apostle dwells at some length on the believer's mystical death to sin in Rom. vi. In ver. 2 he says, "We who died to sin, how shall we any longer live therein?" In ver. 11, drawing a parallel between Christ's being alive and the believer's spiritual life, he says, "Even so, reckon ye also yourselves to be dead unto sin, but alive unto God in Christ Jesus." Then, as a commentary on the meaning which he attaches to the mystical death of which he has been speaking, and as indicating that he does not consider his Roman readers as perfect, he exhorts them in the following manner (vv. 12–14), "Let not sin, therefore, reign in your mortal body, that ye should obey the lusts thereof: neither present your members unto sin as instruments of unrighteousness; but present yourselves unto God as alive from the dead, and your members as instruments of righteousness unto God. For sin shall not have dominion over you: for ye are not under law, but under grace." The same idea as that which Paul expresses in the passages which we have quoted is found also in 1 Pet. ii. 24, "Who His own self bare our sins in His own body on the tree, that we, being dead unto sins, might live unto righteousness."

We have been arguing as if the apostle's expression in the passage before us were simply *dead to sins*. His actual words, as we render them in the 1st verse, are, "Who are dead to your trespasses and sins." This is shortened in the 5th verse to "Dead to our trespasses." But we believe no argument against our view can be based on this variation of phraseology. It is very generally conceded that it is impossible to draw any distinction which is of universal application between παραπτώματα and ἁμαρτίαι. Perhaps they are used together in the 1st verse merely for the sake of emphasis.

Col. ii. 13 is admittedly parallel to the passage we are considering. Our Revisers have accordingly rendered it in the same way. But the general argument which we have employed leads us to translate thus: "You also who are dead to your trespasses and the uncircumcision of your flesh—you did He quicken together with Him," etc. The connection of these words with the preceding context closely resembles the connection between chs. i. and ii. in Ephesians. In the last clause of ver. 12 mention is made of God having raised up Christ from the dead. The spiritual resurrection of the Colossian converts comes in very naturally in ver. 13, "You also," etc. Many commentators have been misled as to the teaching of this verse by the credit they attached to MSS. in which the preposition ἐν occurred before τοῖς παραπτώμασι. The Revisers have taken away any argument which the presence of this particle might furnish by excluding it from their accepted Greek text. This Greek text we accept as correct, and as warranted by the best MS. authority. We note, in passing, that instead of ταῖς ἁμαρτίαις in Eph. ii. 1, we have in this passage in Colossians τῇ ἀκροβυστίᾳ τῆς σαρκός. This may be for the sake of emphasis, as we suggested in connection with the use of παραπτώμασι and ἁμαρτίαις in the verse in Ephesians.

1 Tim. v. 6 may seem to some inconsistent with the views we have expressed. We have said that the view which the Revisers express in their translation of Eph. ii. 1 is not warranted by any other passage in the New Testament. But at first sight this verse in Timothy seems to refute our assertion. The Revisers thus translate the verse in question: "But she that

giveth herself to pleasure is dead while she liveth." The Rev. H. D. M. Spence, M.A., in Ellicott's *Commentaries on the New Testament*, says that here we have a thoroughly Pauline thought, and that the widow who could so forget her sorrow and her duty is spoken of as a living *corpse*, while her believing sister is described as *living*. And he quotes from the *Antigone* of Sophocles words which, he thinks, convey an illustrative sense: "I do not consider that such an one lives, but I regard him as a living corpse." He also refers to Rev. iii. 1 as justification of his view, "These things saith he that hath the seven Spirits of God, and the seven stars: I know thy works, that thou hast a name, that thou livest and art dead." In making this quotation I have omitted the pronoun *thou*, which the Revisers insert before *art dead*. This pronoun is not called for by the Greek, and is evidently used to support a dogmatic position which we consider false.

The passage from Sophocles cannot be regarded as giving any actual support to the view which it is adduced to support. It merely declares that one who spends his time in a particular way cannot be said truly to live. He never finds that true happiness which right living is fitted to impart. He may as well be a corpse so far as true living is concerned. It is ridiculous to adduce a poetical passage of this kind as illustrative of the state in which unconverted men are, or as throwing any light on Pauline theology. It seems to bear only an outward resemblance to the passage in Timothy, and that only if we regard the rendering of the Revisers as correct. The absurdity of such an illustration will appear if we apply a simple test. Suppose the poet were to set before us the case of one who, in his opinion, was living a right life, would we call that an example of a God-fearing, converted man? Sophocles, I am afraid, will not do much to enable us to understand Pauline theology.

The passage in Rev. iii., when rightly explained, will do as little as the passage from Sophocles to show that, either in the passage in Ephesians or in that in Colossians, the apostle is referring to unconverted men. It is part of our Lord's message to the Church in Sardis. The members of that Church were not in the position of unconverted men, but they were in a very low spiritual state. They are half living and half dead. That was their reputation, their ὄνομα. This is clear from what follows: "Be thou faithful, and stablish the things that remain which were ready to die," etc. This language would not have been used if they had been in the position of unconverted men.

But while no illustrative weight can be attached to the quotation from Sophocles, and while we believe that the passage quoted from Revelation, rightly understood, gives no countenance to the idea that either in Eph. ii. 1 or in Col. ii. 13 the apostle is giving a description of unconverted men, we believe that the passage in Timothy, which these quotations were intended more immediately to illustrate, is not accurately rendered by the Revisers any more than the passages in Ephesians or Colossians which we have been examining. The Greek words are ἡ δὲ σπαταλῶσα ζῶσα τέθνηκε. The meaning of the apostle is misrepresented by taking ζῶσα along with τέθνηκε. It should be taken along with ἡ σπαταλῶσα, which, though in form a participle, is here to be taken as a noun (see Winer, sec. xlv. 7). The passage should have been translated thus: "But she who lives a pleasure-seeker has died." The apostle is contrasting two classes of widows. The one class seeks comfort in the fellowship and service of God, and the other gives herself to pleasure. He says of the first, that she has her hope set on God—$ἤλπικεν ἐπὶ Θεόν$. He says of the other, she has died—$τέθνηκε$. Her spiritual life has become extinct. "Now she that is a widow indeed, and desolate, hath her hope set on God, and continueth in supplications and prayers night and day; but she who lives a pleasure-seeker has died." The fact that she gives herself to a life of pleasure shows that her spiritual life has become extinct, if she ever had any. The idea of the apostle in this verse is, therefore, very different from that which the Revisers attach to Eph. ii. 1 and Col. ii. 13.

But there may still lurk in some minds the impression that all dubiety has not yet been removed from the apostle's words in those passages which we have been passing in review. It may be said a man must have been dead before he can be said to have been quickened; if a man has been quickened at conversion, the inference cannot be resisted that he must previously have been dead. And what more natural than to speak of the unrenewed man as dead, and of the believer as made alive? There cannot be any doubt that this argument has influenced the Revisers and interpreters generally. But a little consideration will enable us to expose its fallacy. We must keep carefully before our minds the fact that, in describing the believer's experience, Paul keeps close to the parallel between that experience and the transition through which our Lord passed from His humiliation to His exaltation. There was nothing in our Lord's history corresponding to man's natural state. The apostle begins with our Lord's death, and draws the parallel from that point. There are two sides to the great change of conversion. It is first a death and then a life. The sinner dies to sin and then becomes alive to God. The old man is slain; and this, in Paul's theology, corresponds to the fact of our Lord's death. There is a parallel at that point. Then there is a quickening by the implantation of new feelings and desires; and this corresponds to our Lord's reanimation after death. After that there comes the active obedience of the new man, corresponding to the fact of our Lord's actual leaving of the tomb and entering upon His state of exaltation. Finally, there is the high honour of being made a member of the divine family and exalted to high rank, corresponding to the glory which Christ enjoys in heaven, and carrying with it the potency and hope of sharing with Him that glory. It would be altogether un-Pauline and un-Christian to attempt to find any correspondence between the sinner's natural state and anything in the history of our Lord.

We have gone far beyond our original intention. That was to point out in a few sentences the inaccuracy of the rendering of Eph. ii. 1 by our Revisers and others. We found, however, that the inaccuracy was much more extensive than we at first imagined, and actually extended to the whole sentence. There was nothing for it, if we were to do full justice to the apostle's words, but to recast the whole sentence in English. Then we found that the misconception of Paul's meaning in the passage in Ephesians was supported by misconceptions elsewhere. We were forced to deal with these misconceptions in order that our interpretation might be placed on a solid basis. We trust that we have sufficiently vindicated our main position.

The long parenthesis in Ephesians, including the 2nd and 3rd verses, contains the apostle's description of the state in which both Gentiles and Jews were before their conversion. The 2nd verse applies entirely to Gentiles, of whom the Ephesians were a fair type. They were filled with the spirit of the time, and were Satanic in character. They were thus, according to a Hebrew idiom, sons of disobedience. This last expression naturally leads the apostle to pass on to the case of the Jews. He admits that they were no better than the Gentiles. The testimony of contemporary history bears out the accuracy of Paul's words. They indulged in fleshly lusts, and were mental anarchists. They were immoral in their lives and disloyal in their relations to God, and were, according to another Hebrew idiom, children of wrath, even as the rest—meaning thereby Gentiles. There was thus, so far as their moral and spiritual state was concerned, no difference between Jews and Gentiles before they became Christians. This being so, the apostle feels that he must class his kinsmen and Gentiles together, as, in their unconverted state, *all under sin*. He does not make any exception of his own case, for, though he had not been an immoral man as Saul, the Jew and persecutor, there was so much that was bad in his heart that, in the spirit of Christian courtesy and humility, he speaks as if he had no right to claim superiority over his brethren.

This explanatory parenthesis enables the apostle to change ὑμᾶς of the 1st verse into ἡμᾶς in the 4th and 5th. As he was writing to Ephesian Gentiles, he was under the necessity of using ὑμᾶς; but after showing that there was no practical difference between Jew and Gentile, and when wishing to speak of both, he naturally uses ἡμᾶς. He is anxious to show that both alike have been made partakers of God's grace. Both Gentile and Jewish converts owed their present advantageous position and their future hopes to God's sovereign love. At the 4th verse the apostle begins anew the sentence which he broke off at the end of the 1st verse for the parenthetical explanation of the 2nd and 3rd verses, and puts the result of his explanation in the sentence thus anew begun. In accordance with this fact we translate δέ by *I say*. The Revisers have so translated this particle in 2 Cor. v. 8, and they often use the English expression in question when there is no such particle in the Greek.

But this interpretation of δέ, in a resumptive thought, is so well established in Greek usage that we believe no objection can be made to its being so translated here. The apostle brings down the word Θεός from ch. i. 17. This word is the subject of the verbs συνεζωοποίησε, συνήγειρε, and συνεκάθισεν. These verbs, as we have said, all require the words τῷ Χριστῷ—with Christ—to complete the ideas which they are used to express. This can be seen from our translation as well as from the Greek. But what are the ideas which the apostle wishes to express? Does he refer to the status of believers on earth or in heaven? The answer must be to the former. They share on earth a life and honours such as belonged to Christ after He was raised from the dead. The apostle delights to draw a parallel between Christ's resurrection life and the believer's converted state. And this parallel is of the nature of a prophecy, that all the disabilities of the believer's present state will be removed in heaven, and that he will share the glory which Christ now enjoys there.

We have thus tried, we trust not vainly, to indicate what seems to us the true meaning of the passage which has been under consideration.

*Note.*— The phrase ἐν τοῖς ἐπουρανίοις occurs *five* times in this Epistle, and is not met with elsewhere in the New Testament. We have not seen any translation or explanation of it which we can accept as satisfactory. The rendering *in the heavenlies* conveys no definite idea. The Revisers of 1611 do not seem very decided. They put in the text *in heavenly places*, and in the margin, as an alternative, *things*. They, however, find that they cannot render vi. 12 in this way, and translate *in high places*. The Revisers of 1881 accept *in the heavenly places*—*places*, of course, being printed in italics in both versions, as the Greek has no equivalent word. This is the common way of understanding the phrase. It seems to be accepted almost as an axiom that it designates *place*.

Why this view should have been so persistently taken we do not quite see. It is fortunate that the phrase occurs so often in this Epistle. This should be helpful in determining its meaning. We may safely assume that it is used in the same sense in all instances of its occurrence. And therefore, to use an arithmetical phrase, we shall have to try and reduce these instances to a common denominator. We do not see why italics should be required at all in translating the phrase. It is not necessary to assume that the word ἐπουρανίοις is neuter. It may be taken as masculine. And so taken, it seems to us that the phrase presents a better sense. Wolf in his *Curæ Philologicæ, in loco,* ii. 6, says: " *Inter cœlites*, seu *cœli incolas* vertit Cl. Œderus, *l.c.* p. 680, quamvis cum iis, qui dona et bona cœlestia malunt non valde litigandum putet." This is the nearest approach to our rendering which we have seen. It is the only other, so far as we know, which takes ἐπουρανίοις as masculine.

The idea of great height is inherent in the word *heaven*. "As the heaven is high above the earth."[1] "The heaven for height, and the earth for depth, and the heart of kings is unsearchable."[2] And in this same Epistle, "He that descended is the same also that ascended far above all the heavens, that He might fill all things."[3] While the word οὐρανός thus conveys this idea of great height, the preposition ἐπ' adds intensity to that idea. It seems, therefore, natural enough to ascribe to the word thus compounded the secondary meaning which we ascribe to it in our translation, *among the most exalted*. Let us see how this translation fits into the five different passages in which the phrase occurs. We shall take these in their order.

1. Ch. i. 3: "Blessed be the God and Father of our Lord Jesus Christ, who had blessed us in every spiritual blessing *among the most exalted* in Christ." We can make no sense of the apostle's words if we accept the translation *in the heavenly places*. The expression *in Christ* must be taken along with the words *in every spiritual blessing*. The apostle is thanking God for all the spiritual blessings bestowed on him and his fellow-believers in Christ. And he gratefully recognises the high honour to which all believers are raised. He and his readers are among this honoured class. They share the honour bestowed on Christ.

2. Ch. i. 20: "Which He (God) wrought in Christ, when He raised Him from the dead, and made Him to sit at His right hand among the most exalted." Here *the most exalted* must mean those brought to

[1] Ps. ciii. 11.   [2] Prov. xxv. 3.   [3] Eph. iv. 10.

heaven by Christ. Among these Christ sits, according to the words of His own promise, "He that overcometh, I will give to him to sit down with Me in My throne, as I also overcame and sat down with My Father in His throne."[1]

3. Ch. ii. 6 : "Made us sit with Him among the most exalted in Christ Jesus." This is that instance of the occurrence of the phrase to explain which we have been induced to refer to all the other instances of its use. Here *the most exalted* must be taken, as in the last example, to mean redeemed men. The words *in Christ Jesus* further describes them, to distinguish them from those afterwards to be mentioned who occupy a bad eminence.

4. Ch. iii. 10 : "To the intent that now unto the principalities and the powers among the most exalted might be made known, through the Church, the manifold wisdom of God," etc. Here the phrase refers to rulers and those exercising the highest authority among men. In the preceding context Paul is speaking of the great grace bestowed upon him when he was appointed to preach among the Gentiles the unsearchable riches of Christ. He received this grace (1) to make all men understand the mystery of the gospel, and (2) to make known to those in authority the manifold wisdom of God. It was part of the commission which the apostle received that he was to speak of Christ before men of the highest rank. When Ananias demurred to visit Saul of Tarsus because of the evil reports he had heard regarding him, the Lord said unto him, "Go thy way; for he is a chosen vessel unto Me to bear My name before the Gentiles, and kings, and the children of Israel."[2] In another chapter of the

[1] Rev. iii. 21. [2] Acts ix. 15.

Acts we have a commentary on this aspect of Paul's mission: "So on the morrow, when Agrippa was come, and Bernice, with great pomp, and they were entered into the place of hearing, with the chief captains, and the principal men of the city, at the command of Festus, Paul was brought in."[1] To these principalities and powers—these most exalted men—Paul sought to make known the manifold wisdom of God.

5. Ch. vi. 12: "For our wrestling is not against flesh and blood, but against the principalities, against the powers, against the world-rulers of this darkness, against the spiritualities of wickedness among the most exalted." Here the apostle enumerates all the adverse influences against which Christians had to contend in his day. These were of two kinds. (1) The governing authorities. These sought to persecute the saints, and lead them to abandon the cause of Christ. It was difficult to induce men to become Christians and remain steadfast, when they knew that they exposed themselves to death. Then (2) there were the evil spirits of the nether world always exercising a malign influence, and co-operating with unbelieving princes and potentates. Two expressions are employed by the apostle in each case to describe these adverse influences: in the first case, the principalities and powers; in the second, the world-rulers of this darkness and the spiritualities of wickedness. These opponents of Christ's people were among *the most exalted*, but their eminence was conspicuously bad. In the words which follow those we have commented on, the apostle exhorts his readers to avail themselves of all the assistance offered to them in the gospel, and to stand fast against all their spiritual foes.

[1] Acts xxv. 23.

## VI

# THINGS WHICH MAKE SALVATION CERTAIN

### AN EXEGETICAL STUDY

Καὶ (τὰ) ἐχόμενα σωτηρίας.—HEB. vi. 9.

"And things that accompany salvation."
—*Authorised Version* and *Revised Version*.

DOES this translation, which our Revisers of 1881 have copied from their predecessors of 1611, correctly represent the Greek words? The Revisers themselves are in doubt on the point. Instead of the word "accompany," the English section give us, in the margin, the alternative rendering, "are near to." The American company, on the other hand, think the marginal rendering should be "which belong to." This diversity of opinion is somewhat perplexing to the ordinary reader, but is quite in accordance with the exegetical history of the passage. The opinion of interpreters has all along been much divided. Some have even held that ἐχόμενα is pleonastic, while others have thought that σωτηρίας refers, not to eternal salvation, but to temporal deliverance. These views are now exploded, and no exegete of the present day would think of expressing them. All modern expositors understand σωτηρίας to refer to the salvation which the gospel brings, and all try to give ἐχόμενα its full, natural meaning. The word σωτηρία, wherever it occurs, must be interpreted in accordance with the trend of the writer's thought and the nature of the subject; and there can be no doubt what is its meaning here.

We may make another remark before we go further. The whole of the verse is antithetical. But how is the antithesis to be defined? Ebrard says, "᾽Εχόμενα σωτηρίας forms only the general antithesis to κατάρας ἐγγύς." Westcott says, "The phrase is parallel with, and yet distinct from, κατάρας ἐγγύς." We do not quite see what this means. Dr. William Lindsay says, "᾽Εχόμενα σωτηρίας is obviously a contrast to κατάρας ἐγγύς." So Farrar and others. Now, this view of the limits of the antithesis seems to us too narrow, and lacking in exegetical insight. The writer is evidently contrasting the whole character and destiny of those who fall away, as depicted in the preceding context, with what he believes to be true of his readers. The 7th and 8th verses contain simply an illustration, drawn from nature, to enforce his teaching. To seize upon a phrase in that illustration, and make that one of the limbs of the antithesis, is not exegesis.

The views of interpreters classify themselves under four heads.

1. That which accepts the rendering of our English versions. This view is supported by such authors as Owen, Doddridge, Whitby, and many others. It is vague and indefinite. "To accompany" is to go along with, as a companion or associate. The word leaves us quite in the dark as to whether we are to understand by salvation something enjoyed in this world or

in the next. But this vagueness is looked upon by the votaries of this view as an element essential to the exposition of the words. Delitzsch says, "The expression is intentionally ambiguous or vague." Ebrard says, "The expression is left purposely indefinite, and it is wrong to attempt to find one or another precise sense." These statements are surely made in oblivion of the fact that the 10th verse makes it indubitable that our author was thinking of salvation as something to be obtained in the future world. If that be so, then the things that accompany salvation must be the enjoyments of heaven, exemption from sin and all the miseries associated with it, the beatific vision, communion with Christ and all redeemed men, and the perfect realisation of all that our ransomed nature can desire. But this cannot be the meaning. The sacred penman is evidently referring to personal qualities, at the time of his writing distinguishing his readers, and therefore connected with this world. There are some who make "conversion" and "salvation" synonymous terms. It looks as if our Revisers did not wish to express any opinion on the point. Those who hold this view will, of course, take the words to mean that when a man is converted, or *saved*, as they express it, there are found in him the ordinary characteristics of Christians. But that does not express the force of our author's words. He evidently wishes to comfort his readers by the expression of his conviction that they were on the way to salvation, and were not among the number of those who fall away after having accepted the gospel for a time.

2. The view which interprets the words before us

by some such phrase as that which the English company put in the margin—"are near to," "are nearer to," "are bordering on," "are very near to," salvation. So the Vulgate, Œcumenius,[1] Luther, Castalio, Bengel, Moses Stuart, Dr. William Lindsay, and others. Strictly speaking, "nearness" can refer only to time or place. Both ideas are here excluded by the nature of the case. The sacred penman is not speaking of salvation as a thing near or remote, but of certain spiritual qualities which he believed belonged to his readers. These qualities could not be spoken of in any strict sense as near, or nearer, salvation. They might be described as bringing their possessors nearer to salvation; but that is not the idea expressed by this translation now in question. And even if that had been the idea of the sacred writer, it would not have brought much comfort to his readers in the circumstances. For those thought of as falling away were once supposed to be near salvation! Our author wishes to place his readers on firmer ground than that. The words before us, as translated by our Revisers in the margin, cannot be taken as parallel to Paul's words in Rom. xiii. 12, "Now is our salvation nearer than when we believed." Westcott says, "The construction $\check{\epsilon}\chi\epsilon\sigma\theta\alpha\iota\ \tau\acute{\iota}\nu\sigma\varsigma$ is used of local contiguity in Mark i. 38; of temporal connection, Luke xiii. 33, Acts xx. 15, and xxi. 26." To give point to this critical remark, he should have suggested the rendering, "in touch with salvation." But this would have been as objectionable as any of the phrases with which we have been dealing under this head. It could not have brought any comfort to our author's readers, for the evil in the case of those whom he

---

[1] Œcumenius interprets $\dot{\epsilon}\chi\acute{o}\mu\epsilon\nu\alpha$ by $\dot{\epsilon}\gamma\gamma\dot{\upsilon}\varsigma\ \check{o}\nu\tau\alpha$.

thinks of as falling away is that they lose touch with salvation. And that is the very danger against which the sacred writer seeks to warn them. He wishes to encourage them to perseverance in faithfulness to Christ by the assurance that their salvation was certain, if they so persevered.

3. The view which accords, more or less, with the judgment of the American company, and would translate, "which belong to," "are connected with," "are inseparably connected with," "are akin to," "which partake of the nature of," salvation. So Erasmus, Beza, Piscator, Macknight, Kuinoel, Lünemann, Tholuck, Boothroyd, Darby, Alford, etc. Tholuck's view, as given by his translator, James Hamilton, M.A., is strangely expressed. "'Ἐχόμενα σωτηρίας," he says, "is a classical periphrasis of the adjective notion." He must intend to say, "things of saving virtue." Augustine, writing to Cresconius, expresses his view thus: "Things to which eternal salvation closely adheres." This view seems to us to come very near the author's meaning, though we feel that it fails to bring out an essential feature of the words. The translation is not sufficiently clear, and does not remove all ambiguity from the passage. The words, "which partake of the nature of," confound the means, or antecedents, of salvation with salvation itself. For the same reason, the rendering of Alford—"are akin to"—is also objectionable.

4. The view which adds to the words, "are connected with salvation," some such phrase as "and lead to" it, as necessary to bring out the full sense. So Paræus, Raphelius, Dindorf in his edition of Ernesti on our Epistle, and Dr. A. B. Davidson. Paræus says, "Literally, containing salvation, or

contiguous to salvation; for ἐχόμενα is properly used of those things that follow one another so as mutually to touch, like adjoining buildings. He (our author) understands, therefore, the necessary antecedents to salvation, such as faith, conversion, patience, constancy, and perseverance. Those who have these, and maintain them, are certain of salvation." Paræus does not put into his translation all that he has in his exposition. In fact, his translation and his exposition do not correspond with one another. He is apparently controlled by tradition in translating, but his exegetical instinct leads him to express the whole truth when expounding. The words of Raphelius are, "Things which carry salvation with them, which are connected with it, and make for it." Dindorf says, "As we view it, τὰ ἐχόμενα σωτηρίας means 'things which bring salvation, and secure it.'" That satisfies the critical conscience. Many interpreters seem to have had the conviction that this idea: *and leading to it*, is involved in the phrase, but have not been able to express it. With this method of bringing out the meaning of the words before us we cordially agree. The phrase used by the sacred writer is a pregnant one. We cannot rid ourselves of the conviction that when any part of the verb ἔχω is used in connection with eternal life, or salvation, there is inseparably connected with it the idea of security and certainty. That idea should certainly be expressed here. Let us glance at a few passages in illustration of our meaning. John iii. 16, "God so loved the world, that He gave His only-begotten Son, that whosoever believeth in Him should not perish, but *have* (ἔχῃ) eternal life. For God sent not the Son into the world to judge the world, but that the world should be saved through Him." The word "have" here has the meaning of "obtain, and be sure of." More definite still is the 36th verse of the same chapter, "He that believeth on the Son *hath* (ἔχει) eternal life; but he that obeyeth not the Son shall not see life, but the wrath of God abideth on him." Here the force of "hath" is undoubtedly "shall infallibly obtain." This is clear from the antithesis stated in the second and third clauses of the verse. Then, in this same gospel, ch. v. 24, the words occur, "He that heareth My word, and believeth Him that sent Me, *hath* (ἔχει) eternal life, and cometh not into judgment, but hath passed out of death into life." This verse needs no special comment. It is a feeble exposition that interprets " hath " in these passages to mean " hath it now." What, then, are the things in the Christian's character that secure his salvation? They are such as faith, a growing hatred of sin and a corresponding love of holiness, a hunger and thirst for the word, a craving for communion with God, and a deepening interest in His cause. And these our author believed that his readers possessed. On the whole, we would prefer, as a rendering of the words, this: "And things that ensure salvation."

# VII

# OUR LORD TROUBLED AND TRIUMPHANT

### A Lecture

"Now is My soul troubled; and what shall I say? Father, save Me from this hour? But for this cause came I unto this hour. Father, glorify thy name. There came therefore a voice out of heaven—'I have both glorified it, and will glorify it again.' The multitude, therefore, that stood by, and heard it, said that it had thundered. Others said, 'An angel hath spoken to Him.' Jesus answered and said, 'This voice hath not come for My sake, but for your sakes. Now is the judgment of this world: now shall the prince of this world be cast out. And I, if I be lifted up from the earth, will draw all men unto Myself.' But this He said, signifying by what manner of death He should die."—JOHN xii. 27–34.

WHAT caused the sudden access of mental anguish with which our Lord was now visited? To answer this question intelligently, we must go back to what our evangelist says about certain Greeks who had come up to Jerusalem to worship at the feast. This is acknowledged on all hands to be necessary. The commonly received opinion regarding these men is, that they were anxious inquirers, who wished to have an opportunity of conversing with Jesus. It is assumed that they had heard much about His doctrine, had become deeply interested in it, and that they craved the advantages of a private interview.

This opinion seems to be founded mainly, if not entirely, upon the *apparently* respectful form of the request. As that request is usually read, it wears the appearance of great modesty. Instead of applying directly to our Lord, they sought to approach Him through one of His disciples. They wished to *see* Jesus. What this really meant cannot be conclusively inferred from the form of words. The term *see* is the same as that employed in the narrative about Zaccheus: "He sought to *see* Jesus, who He was." Much would depend upon the tone and manner of the speakers. They may have assumed an insolent and threatening aspect as they spoke. They may have presented a sinister and suspicious look. The narrative does not certainly make it imperative that we should believe they were actuated by spiritual concern.

There are three circumstances connected with the story, and lying on its very surface, which make us unwilling to acquiesce in the traditional opinion. (1) There is the hesitation of the disciples. Their suspicions were evidently excited. Philip, to whom the request was made, deemed it prudent to consult with Andrew. Why not take them to Jesus at once if they were good and true men, and appeared to be such ? It was only after the two had consulted together that the matter was mentioned to Jesus. It has been suggested that Philip's hesitation arose from our Lord's express assurance, that He had not come except to the lost sheep of the house of Israel. When the Twelve were sent forth to preach after their ordination, they were told not to go into the way of the Gentiles. And these men were Gentiles, not Jews. But we must remember that we have here before us persons who do not belong to the category of Gentiles proper.

They were proselytes to the Jewish faith, and were thus, to a certain extent, identified with the Jewish community. The hesitation of the disciples is not explained by this suggestion. (2) There is no evidence in the narrative that our Lord granted an interview. If the men had been actuated by a right spirit, we can hardly doubt that our Lord would have complied with their wishes. And if the interview had been granted, it is reasonable to think that we would have had some account of it. The matters on which they wished to be informed would have been mentioned, and our Lord's attitude towards them indicated. There is the profoundest silence in the narrative after we are informed that Andrew and Philip told Jesus. There is evidently a material difference between the case of these men and that of Zaccheus. Zaccheus was an eminently good man, and what he had heard of Christ filled him with the deepest admiration. There is no evidence, apart from the dubious form of their request, that these men had any sympathy with Jesus, or cared anything about His doctrine. They were most probably fanatics, who had heard of the bitter feeling which prevailed among the Jews against our Lord, and who had become more Jewish, in this respect, than the Jews themselves, and only sought to see Jesus that they might assassinate Him. (3) The request of these men threw our Lord into great mental distress. Everyone admits the connection between this distress and the visit of these Greeks. Now, our Lord's distress could not have been due to honest religious interest on the part of these men. There must have been something sinister about their whole conduct. They must have been bent upon laying violent hands upon our Lord there and then.

It is only on this supposition that it is possible to explain this otherwise inexplicable passage in our Gospel. Our Lord was now filled with distress because He feared premature death. As death in such a form as that now threatened, and at such a time, was inconsistent with what His Father had revealed to Him as to the manner and time of His death, and as it seemed to make it impossible that all that was written in the Law of Moses and in the Prophets and Psalms concerning Him could be fulfilled, we can understand this sudden outburst of mental trouble. Our Lord all along was anxious to do all that the Father had given Him to do. Was His career to be cut short before all had been done?

We cannot fairly set aside this supposition by appealing to the statement of our evangelist, that these Greeks had come up to Jerusalem to worship at the feast. The Jews who clamoured for our Lord's crucifixion, and ultimately gained their object, had come up to the Holy City for the same purpose. We cannot predict what misguided men, under the influence of fanaticism and passion, will do. The Greeks are a hot-blooded people, and assassination is not a thing unheard of in the history of their nation. Are we reminded that we are explaining this passage by the aid of a supposition? So far as that goes, the opinion that these Greeks were anxious inquirers is but a supposition too; and we do not think it is a supposition so well founded as that which we have brought forward. Our supposition, when stated, comes very near to a demonstration.

Our Lord's present distress cannot be accounted for by His fear of death. Had He been actually afraid of death, it could have been justly said that He had less courage in this respect than has been shown by many of His followers since. He all along knew that He was to die. It was His fixed and unalterable purpose to give His life a ransom for many. "Therefore doth My Father love Me," we have found Him saying in this Gospel before, "because I lay down My life, that I might take it again. No man taketh it from Me, but I lay it down of Myself." "And it came to pass, when the time was come that He should be received up, He steadfastly set His face to go to Jerusalem." It is to our mind simply impossible to think that our Lord's present distress was caused by the near prospect of death. He was always willing to die, but He did not wish to die till all that had been written concerning Him had been fulfilled. It was premature death, which would leave His work incomplete, that He dreaded.

In His distress our Lord betook Himself to His Father in prayer. But He hesitated, for a brief period, as to how He should express Himself. What was He to say? Was His prayer to be, "Father, save Me from this hour"? That language He could not use. It would imply a want of confidence in His Father's goodness and providence. He had been brought into His present position by the divine leading, just as He had been led by the Spirit into the wilderness to be tempted of the devil. God must have had a special reason for bringing about the present circumstances. And He felt that it was His duty to acquiesce. "Though He were a Son, yet learned He obedience by the things which He suffered." This was a new test of His filial confidence. We must remember that our Lord placed Himself, for the accomplishment of our redemption, under all the conditions of ordinary humanity. He had to learn, as we need to do, His Father's will in connection with the leadings of Providence. And we need not be surprised that He found it difficult sometimes to discover what that will was. The result of His mediation, before His Father's throne at this time, was to dissipate the cloud which had settled down upon His soul. Hence His submissive words, " Father, glorify Thy name." That is, " Carry out Thy will concerning Me. I am ready to submit to all that Thou art pleased to appoint for Me. And Thou knowest how to defeat the machinations of wicked men, and to bring to pass what Thou hast ordained. I cheerfully resign myself into Thy hands."

It is exceedingly probable that this was the occasion referred to in Hebrews, where it speaks of the Lord offering up prayers and supplications, with strong crying and tears, to Him that was *able to save Him from death*. The phrase is suggestive, and, on our supposition, looks like an undesigned coincidence. It does not follow that both passages do not refer to the same period, because the account of our evangelist is so meagre.

The people (more correctly, the multitude) must have heard this prayer, though it does not seem to have been a common thing with our Lord to pray to His Father in the hearing of the unsympathetic crowd. His evident reason for presenting His prayer in the hearing of the people was to secure that their attention should be called to the answer. He wished to convince them that there was perfect understanding between Him and the Father, and that He had made no claim which the Father did not endorse. The answer to His prayer came in the words, " I have both glorified it, and will glorify it again." That this answer was given in articulate sounds, seems indisputable. But what did it mean? It meant that the Father had exercised a guardian care over His Son in the past. He had opened up a way of escape from all the dangers to which He had hitherto been exposed. He had, at the beginning of His public ministry, enabled Him to escape from the enraged villagers of Nazareth; and He had more recently, on two occasions, enabled Him to escape out of the hands of the Jews. All this had been done because His hour had not yet come. It could not be that He should die before His work was done. But the voice from heaven also meant that He would be delivered from the fanaticism of these Greeks. Their evil intentions would be frustrated, and all that the Father had appointed for Him would be fulfilled. Had Jesus been put to death now, His work would not have been completed. And these Greeks being His murderers, His death could not have been looked upon as a *legal sacrifice*. To constitute His death such a sacrifice, He must be brought to the altar through the agency of the chief priests. It is not without significance, in this connection, that it is written, " Judas, having received a band of men and officers from the chief priests and Pharisees, cometh thither with lanterns, and torches, and weapons." " He was led as a lamb to the slaughter."

Some of the multitude who stood by, when they heard the voice from heaven, said it thundered; others said an angel was speaking to Him. It was very much as it was with the vision which Saul of Tarsus had on the way to Damascus. The persecutor distinctly heard the words spoken; those who were with him heard a sound, but could not discriminate the words. Our Lord explained that the voice came solely for the sake of the multitude. He had already obtained, in His inward calm, evidence that His prayer was answered. He could say now, as He said at the grave of Lazarus, "I knew that Thou hearest Me always: but because of the people which stand by I said it, that they may believe that Thou hast sent Me." The whole scene was so arranged as to encourage them to believe on Him.

This was a critical time in our Lord's earthly life, but it was also a critical time in the history of the world. Our Lord saw in the spirit of these Greeks the fact of His rejection by the Gentile world. The Jews and Gentiles are terms used in the New Testament to describe the whole of mankind. The Jews had already indicated their hostility to Him, and their rejection of Him. This rejection by the Jews was followed by the rejection of the Gentiles. Thus, by the spirit manifested by the Greeks, it was made manifest that the whole world was set in array against Christ. All nations are to share in the benefits of His death, and all nations, through their representatives, had a share in compassing His death.

It seemed at one time as if the forces of evil were to triumph, and as if the plans and purposes of Heaven were to be thwarted. But this prospect of the triumph of evil was short-lived. What at first looked like a victory was to end in ignominious defeat. The devil's seeming triumph was really the Lord's victory. The power of man's great enemy would be destroyed; the prince of this world would be cast out. There is a ring of triumph in the words which our Lord here uses, "Now shall the prince of this world be cast out." The enemies of Christ have often imagined that they have prevailed against Christ.

But He that sitteth in the heavens laughed; the Lord had them in derision. No weapon formed against God can prosper.

In this triumphant strain our Lord continues: "And I, if I be lifted up from the earth, will draw all men unto Myself. But this He said signifying by what manner of death He should die." Here our Lord speaks again, in His wonted language, about the mode of His death. His fears have been removed. He is now satisfied that He will not die till all has been fulfilled. The providential guardianship of His Father will keep Him safe till His time has come, and till all that has been given Him to do has been accomplished.

There is no evidence here of our Lord's fear of mere death—He thinks only of the grand results that were to follow from His death. "I, if I be lifted up from the earth, will draw all men unto Myself." His death would accomplish what His life had failed to secure. While He lived on earth men had hated and despised Him. He was a root out of a dry ground, and when they saw Him there was no beauty in Him that they should desire Him. There were times when the people were drawn towards Him for a brief period, but this was speedily followed by reaction. His death would make a favourable change. Men would be induced to think of Him in a different way. The purity of His life, the love and unselfishness which He manifested, the divine nature of His doctrines, and especially the cruel death He was to die, would evoke human sympathy; and that, in turn, would awaken admiration, faith, and love. As matter of fact, there is nothing which touches the heart of the sinner like the story of the Cross. When every other appeal fails, this can find its way to the conscience.

The love which breathes from the Cross kindles love in the sinner's soul.

The word *all* here must not be taken absolutely, as meaning that all men individually were to be drawn to Christ after His death. That cannot be the meaning, for we know that, as matter of fact, all men are not drawn to Him. In every age there have been some that have rejected Him and turned their backs upon Him. The evident meaning of the word is, that there will be drawn to Him some men out of every kindred and race — Jews as well as Gentiles. This, we know, has been done. Wherever the gospel has been preached some have been found to accept it. And our Lord's prediction here is receiving, in our day, a more complete fulfilment than at any previous period since His death. Even the Jews, who have so long treated Him with hostility, are beginning to speak of Him with admiration. The cause of the gospel is not a failure. However the careless may treat it, however the wise men of the world may regard it, its triumph is the one outstanding fact in the history of the world at the present day.

"Unto Him that loved us, and washed us from our sins in His own blood, and hath made us kings and priests unto God and His Father; to Him be glory and dominion for ever and ever. Amen."

# VIII

# THE GETHSEMANE CUP—WHAT WAS IT?

"O My Father, if it be possible, let this cup pass away from Me: nevertheless not as I will, but as Thou wilt."—MATT. xxvi. 39.

"The cup which the Father hath given Me, shall I not drink it?"—JOHN xviii. 11, last clause.

ON this question two different opinions have contended for acceptance.

I. The majority of interpreters have held that by this cup we are to understand the terrible ordeal of the Cross. Our Lord had come into this world, assuming our mortal flesh, for the express purpose of dying for men, and, during the whole course of His life and ministry on earth up to this time, had spoken of His death as something which lay before Him, and to which He was ready cheerfully to submit; but, we are told, when the hour of His sufferings actually approached He shrank from the prospect. His heart was overwhelmed by an unspeakable horror, which found expression in the agony of the garden. There was something inconceivably awful in the thought of having to bear the load of the world's sin. But this our Lord did not fully realise till brought face to face with it. (1) It is a fatal objection to this view that it presents our Lord in a most vacillating light. What! are we to suppose that He now wished to abandon the great purpose for which He came into the world, and to stultify all that He had previously said and done? He told His disciples that He had a baptism to be baptized with, and that He was greatly straitened till it was accomplished. When the time came that He should be offered up, He steadfastly set His face to go to Jerusalem, where He expected to be put to death. Is it consistent with our Lord's character to suppose that He repented at the very last? This opinion, we humbly think, seriously dishonours Him. The words of John xii. 27–34 and of Heb. v. 7, refer to an occasion totally different from the scene in Gethsemane. (2) But another objection, equally fatal to this opinion, is drawn from the words which our Lord used in His prayer regarding this cup. These words slightly vary in the different evangelists, but they all convey the same meaning. Take those found in Mark: "Abba, Father, all things are possible unto Thee; take away this cup from Me." Was it possible for God, in harmony with the plan of redemption, to allow Christ to evade the Cross? It is evident that we must interpret the cup to mean something which it was possible for God to do, while at the same time yielding up Christ to die for us. Christ could not be saved from the Cross, and at the same time offer Himself as a sacrifice for sin.

II. A large number of expositors, dissatisfied with the opinion which we have been examining, believe that our Lord was now in a condition so physically reduced that He was afraid of dying before He could reach the Cross. He shrank, it is alleged, not from death on the Cross, but from death in Gethsemane.

This view is supported by such arguments as these—
(1) Luke, in his account of the scene in the garden, mentions that an angel came from heaven to strengthen Him. Hence it is argued He must have suffered from physical weakness. But this inference does not follow. The strength imparted to Him may have been, and, undoubtedly, was, of a spiritual nature, to enable Him to bear what the Father had appointed for Him. Had the strength imparted by the angel been of a physical nature, the result must have been to relieve His agony and reassure Him. No such result was, however, produced. It is immediately added that, "*being in agony, He prayed more earnestly*; and His sweat was as it were great drops of blood falling down to the ground." The strengthening which He received did not, it is evident, mitigate the bitterness of the cup, whatever that was. There is no warrant whatever for the belief that our Lord thought Himself dying. He told His disciples, it is true, that His soul was exceedingly sorrowful, *even unto death*; but evidently this expression is employed merely to mark the intensity of His mental anguish. (2) A further argument in support of this view is, that our Lord did not die in Gethsemane. The reasoning here is what logicians call a vicious circle. It is assumed that Christ prayed to be delivered from premature death, and then, because He did not die in the garden, it is argued that premature death was what He dreaded. (3) A third argument is drawn from the words used by our Lord at the grave of Lazarus, "I know that Thou hearest me always." But such an argument involves a fallacy. Hearing a prayer, and granting the request which such a prayer presents, are not one and the same thing. The terms

which the Lord used implied that He was not certain that His request would be granted. He left Himself in the Father's hands—" Nevertheless, not My will, but Thine, be done." God hears our prayers, but does not always grant what we ask. Paul prayed to be delivered from his thorn in the flesh, but, though his prayer was heard, its request was not granted.

A conclusive objection to this view arises out of John xviii. 11. When Peter smote Malchus, and cut off his right ear, our Lord said to him, " Put up thy sword into the sheath ; the cup which My Father hath given Me, shall I not drink it ? " Clearly the cup was not something removed from our Lord at this time when He was leaving the garden. It seems difficult to escape from this inference, but some boldly say, The cup in the garden, and the cup here referred to, are not one and the same. Such an argument needs no reply. The cup, for the removal of which Christ prayed, must have been something which caused Him intense mental anguish, but something which did not seem to Him to enter into the essence of His mission—something, in short, from which He might escape without setting aside the purpose for which He came into the world. What that was we shall now endeavour to show.

III. We are forced to conclude that by the cup from which our Lord shrank, is to be understood the betrayal, and what might arise out of it. Our Lord knew who it was that was to betray Him. And, looking at the matter from a human standpoint, most awful consequences might spring out of the action of the traitor. There might be serious violence and bloodshed. We believe that these possibilities filled our Lord's mind with alarm and anguish. The considerations which have induced us to adopt this view are these—(1) The directions which Christ gave His disciples as recorded in Luke xxii. 35-38, "And He said unto them, When I sent you without purse, and scrip, and shoes, lacked ye anything? And they said, Nothing. Then said He unto them, But now, he that hath a purse, let him take it, and likewise his scrip: and he that hath no sword, let him sell his garment, and buy one. For I say unto you, That this that is written must yet be accomplished in Me, And He was reckoned among the transgressors: for the things concerning Me have an end. And they said, Lord, behold, here are two swords. And He said unto them, It is enough." These instructions surely pointed to the possibility of great trial and danger. They clearly indicate a fear that the usual channels of hospitality might be closed against the disciples through the hatred that might be excited against them. They indicate also the possibility of their being called upon to struggle for their lives against an infuriated mob. Here we naturally recall what our Lord said to the three whom He appointed to guard Him while He prayed in Gethsemane: "Watch and pray, that ye enter not into temptation." Here we must understand our Lord to refer to physical quite as much as to spiritual danger. It well became them to watch and pray, lest they should be forced to defend their lives against violence. They were set to guard their Master while He prayed, but it would be a most lamentable thing if they were forced to use the sword. They were happily delivered by the providence of God from so painful a necessity. Now, it will be admitted that all these instructions which our Lord gave to His disciples were just such as human prudence might suggest. What concern to avoid collision between the disciples and the armed band is seen in the words, "If ye seek Me, let these go their way"! The armed band was miraculously restrained. When Jesus revealed Himself to them, they went backward and fell to the ground. They seem to have been still under the influence of a strange awe when Peter smote Malchus. We cannot otherwise understand how a scene of violence and bloodshed did not ensue.

(2) John, in connection with the reproof administered to Peter, records the words, "The cup which My Father hath given Me, shall I not drink it!" These words are brought forward by some to prove that it was the Cross which constituted the cup from which our Lord sought to be delivered. See, they say, the drinking of the cup was still a thing in the future. If any argument of this kind could be established, it would be fatal to our view, which is, that our Lord was now drinking the cup which the Father had given Him. But no sound interpreter can be led astray by such an argument. The future tense, as used here, implies moral obligation rather than indicates time. It is so used in many other cases, as, for example, Job ii. 10, "What! shall we receive good at the hand of God, and shall we not receive evil?" Here the future of the verb is used, and yet Job's sufferings were not in the future, but actually upon him. But (3) the conduct of Judas must have caused our Lord intense pain. Can any one doubt that He wished, if it were possible, that He should be delivered to death without the intervention of Judas? That disciple had been dear to Him as the others had been. Then there was the

possibility of the disciples losing all control of themselves when they saw the baseness of the traitor. Besides, (4) there were possibilities of outrage on the part of those who came to apprehend Christ. These were Jews. Might they not be tempted to use violence towards both our Lord and His disciples?

There was surely enough in these possibilities, and in the conduct of Judas, to account for our Lord's intense concern, and to awaken in His mind the desire that the great Disposer of all events might so arrange as to avert from Him so terrible a trial. God answered His prayer, but not in the way He desired. No lives were sacrificed, and no violence was exercised, except by Peter; and that episode speedily terminated with this happy result, that it gave our Lord the opportunity of teaching a most important lesson in Christian morals.

# IX

# IS THE LAST CLAUSE OF JOHN III. 13 GENUINE?

## A Study in Textual Criticism

Καὶ οὐδεὶς ἀναβέβηκεν εἰς τὸν οὐρανόν· εἰ μὴ ὁ ἐκ τοῦ οὐρανοῦ καταβὰς ὁ υἱὸς τοῦ ἀνθρώπου [ὁ ὢν ἐν τῷ οὐρανῷ].—*Textus Receptus*, etc.

"And no man hath ascended into heaven, but He that descended out of heaven—the Son of man."

THE question before us is one of special interest, but, at the same time, one of special difficulty. We have indicated our opinion by leaving the clause in question untranslated. Whether that opinion is well or ill founded must be decided by the reader. We have four classes of authorities to examine. (1) Those which present the clause as it stands in the Textus Receptus, which is that exhibited at the top of this paper. (2) That which reads, ὁ ἐν τῷ οὐρανῷ. (3) Those which read, ὁ ὢν ἐκ τοῦ οὐρανοῦ. (4) And those which omit the clause altogether. The trial of strength is really between the first and the last of these classes. The only undoubted evidence in favour of the second is the Gospel Lectionary 44. The idea that it was the original reading of Codex A rests, as we hope to show, on no evidence whatever. The reading of the third class is supported by the cursives 80 and 88. To these we are now able to add the recently-discovered Sinaitic Syriac palimpsest of the Gospels. This manuscript has the preposition "from" in its full separate form. The fact is interesting and suggestive, but it does not alter our position, that the decision must be in favour of either the first or the fourth class of authorities.

The rules of grammar are not to be forgotten in a case of this kind. It will readily be admitted that our translation entirely satisfies these rules. And we are at a loss to understand what necessity the translators of 1611 and the Revisers of 1881 saw for the supplementary word "even." It is in no way necessary to the sense, and only serves to obscure the apostle's meaning. Our translation is the natural one, according to the Greek *usus loquendi*. So far, therefore, as grammar is concerned, the verse comes to a legitimate termination with the word "man." If the clause was not added by John, its addition since was not called for to meet any grammatical difficulty. Its presence in the text may be due to some supposed logical necessity. When we read over the verse without the last clause, there is a feeling as if the protasis and apodosis did not perfectly balance. We expect a more explicit assertion in the apodosis than we actually find. Westcott and Hort suggest that the clause was probably introduced to correct any misunderstanding that might arise out of the position of ἀναβέβηκεν as coming before καταβάς. The feeling to which we have referred is very much relieved when we remember that εἰ μή does not introduce a directly negative or exceptive proposition. It prepares us rather for a qualification of the statement which preceded it. In this case it gives us to understand that, while no man has ascended into heaven to ascertain God's mind and will, Christ, the Son of God, has become incarnate to reveal to us all that it is necessary for us to know.

The addition of the clause in question makes the verse look like an ill-patched garment. It introduces a contradiction to the clause which states that Christ came down from heaven. Our Lord nowhere else speaks of Himself as being in heaven while He tabernacled upon earth. But those who plead for the retention of the clause use as one of their strong dogmatic arguments that it furnishes a remarkable proof of our Lord's Divinity. While He was on earth, we are told, He was also, through His Divine nature, at the same time in heaven. How can such an exposition be harmonised with such words as these?—John vi. 62, "What, then, if ye should behold the Son of man ascending where He was before?" John xx. 17, "Jesus saith to her, Touch Me not; for I am not yet ascended to the Father." But, further, if we accept the clause, and construe the verse as our English versions do, we have no definite verb in the apodosis. ″Ὤν is a participle, introducing an assumption, but not containing a definite proposition. Our versions get over this difficulty *apparently*, but not *really*, by translating, "who is in heaven." A participial clause, without a definite verb, cannot be treated in this way. The literal rendering is, "who [or, 'He who'], being in heaven." This leaves the verse hanging in the air. We do not see how this grammatical difficulty can be overcome by those who accept the words of the clause in question. This clause should have been followed by some definite verb to satisfy the requirements of grammar.

The following cases illustrate what we mean: John i. 18, "The only-begotten Son, which is (ὁ ὤν) in the bosom of the Father, He hath declared Him"; John vi. 46, "He which is (ὁ ὤν) from God, He hath seen the Father"; John viii. 47, "He that is of God (ὁ ὤν ἐκ τοῦ Θεοῦ) heareth the words of God"; John xviii. 37, "Everyone that is of the truth (πᾶς ὁ ὤν ἐκ τῆς ἀληθείας) heareth My voice." Such examples might easily have been multiplied almost indefinitely. We have confined ourselves exclusively to John's Gospel, in case it should be thought that there is anything in this evangelist's style inconsistent with the position we have taken up. The rules of grammar and the laws of thought alike, require a definite verb after ὁ ὤν. We do not, of course, object to the translation of ὁ ὤν by "he who is" when a definite verb follows; but as there is no such verb in the present case, we regard the rendering of our English versions as illegitimate. We go further, and say that, if we retain the clause, the verse cannot be translated grammatically. From all this we infer that the words in dispute could not have proceeded from John's pen, who is never guilty of a glaring grammatical inaccuracy of this kind. They have all the appearance of having been subsequently imported into the text, and in utter disregard of grammatical rule. They were probably put in the margin of some early exemplar, whose pious possessor wished to express his belief in our Lord's ascension, but who had no thought of adapting his words to the apostle's construction, or any desire to have them regarded as of sacred authority. The grammatical form of the clause stamps it with suspicion, to say the very least.

I. The external evidence in support of the clause is furnished at great length by Tischendorf, Scrivener, and Burgon, who proceed upon the fallacious principle of counting authorities without weighing them. Scrivener says, "The clause is contained in A, E, G, H, K, M, S, U, V, Γ, Δ, Λ, Π, and in all cursives save one." Burgon is more minute, "It is found in every manuscript in the world, except five of bad character; is recognised by *all* the Latin and *all* the Syriac versions, as well as by the Coptic, Æthiopic, Georgian, and Armenian; is either quoted or insisted upon by Origen, Hippolytus, Athanasius, Didymus, Aphraates the Persian, Basil the Great, Epiphanius, Nonnus, pseudo-Dionysius Alex., Eustathius; by Chrysostom, Theodoret, and Cyril, each four times; by Paulus, Bishop of Emesa, Theodore Mops., Amphilochius, Severus, Theodorus Heracl., Basilius Cil., Cosmas, John Damascene, in three places; and four other ancient Greek writers, besides Ambrose, Novatian, Hilary, Lucifer, Victorinus, Jerome, Cassian, Vigilius, Zeno, Marius, Maximus Taur., Capreolus, Augustine," etc. We have not noted the references which Burgon gives to the works of the different ecclesiastical writers here mentioned. This would have occupied too much of our space. They are all given at the foot of p. 133 of *The Revision Revised*—three articles reprinted from the *Quarterly Review*. We have given this evidence in full, to avoid all suspicion of unfairness.

It would be impossible to enter into a full analysis of all this. The versions are the most difficult to dispose of. Some of them must have been made within two hundred years of John's death. But Griesbach, in his *Symbolæ Criticæ*, makes some remarks which go to show that they may not carry with them so much critical weight after all. He asserts that the manuscripts of the Alexandrian and Western recensions (according to his classification) were grossly corrupted in the age immediately succeeding that of the apostles; and that those which he held in the highest esteem bore evidences of being corrupted on every page by marginal *scholia* and interpolations of the Fathers, and contained innumerable and very serious errors. The recently discovered Syriac palimpsest supports Griesbach's remarks in a remarkable manner. From what has reached the public in connection with this interesting manuscript, it would appear that the translator has taken great liberties with the words of the sacred penmen. The clause which we are discussing, if it stood in the copy which he used, was tampered with by him. Instead of making it contradictory to the first clause of the apodosis, he makes it a meaningless repetition of that clause. We do not therefore feel called upon to accept without question the evidence of these ancient versions.

Scrivener quotes Codex A in support of the clause. We are not satisfied that we have here the words of the original scribe. It is admitted on all hands that what was originally written has been erased, and the words of the clause, as they now stand, substituted in its stead. The British Museum authorities have published a beautiful photographic impression of both the Old and New Testament of this most valuable manuscript. Our examination of two different copies of this impression *at this passage* has revealed to us some important and interesting facts. The clause reads, ὁ ὢν ἐν τῷ οὐ͡νῳ—οὐρανῷ being contracted in this way, evidently to avoid encroaching too much on the margin. The evidence of erasure extends from the right-hand side of ὁ to the marginal line, the letters νῳ being clear and distinct, and showing that they were written on a part of the parchment which had not been interfered with by erasing. The O is normal in shape; the ω leans considerably towards the left hand, and thus occupies more space than usual. The N, when carefully examined, shows signs of having been originally a K. There are clear traces of the upper slanting stroke, and what now constitutes the slanting stroke of the N begins about half-way down the left-hand upright stroke, contrary to the scribes' usual way of writing that letter. There is thus not a particle of warrant for the generally received opinion that the original scribe wrote the clause as it now stands, inadvertently omitting ὤν, and having to erase what he had written to get this word inserted. The evidence seems to warrant the conclusion that, as the manuscript originally stood, it contained a reading totally different from anyone that has been transmitted to us. The examination of the passage, as presented in the photographic copies, took us so much by surprise, that we distrusted our own eyesight, and asked two intelligent, sharp-sighted librarians, who knew nothing of Greek, and who could therefore be under no bias, what they saw in the clause. Without any prompting, they at once detected the facts which we have set down. We then began to consider what those facts pointed to, and we found it impossible to resist the conjecture that the original writing was ἐστὶ καὶ τοῦ Θεοῦ.[1] The ε in ἐστί was, of course, as an uncial written Ε. The erasure of the horizontal

---

[1] Possibly Θεοῦ was contracted to Θυ, as in ver. 18.

stroke would not affect the left-hand side of the letter, but only the right-hand one. The whole word, ЄCTI written in uncials, would just fill up the space till we come to the N of ⲰN, which, we have said, bears traces of having originally been a K. We have nothing to go upon in conjecturing that KΑI TOY ΘЄOY completed the verse, except the traces of a K and the extreme probability that a scribe, wishing to make the Divinity of Christ plain, would so write, thinking that the words had been omitted from the copy which he used, or, at all events, should have been there. The words, ἐστὶ καὶ τοῦ Θεοῦ, written in uncials, would just fill up the space to the marginal line, without trenching on the margin; and so we account for the last two letters of οὐρανῷ giving no evidence of erasure. If this way of accounting for the facts which Codex A presents be the true one, then we have succeeded in laying bare a part, at least, of the process by which this passage has been corrupted. No one can say this is not, at least, a plausible account of the facts. It rounds off the verse with a definite verb, the want of which appears to have been a stumbling-block to many, and seems to supply the matter necessary to balance the protasis and apodosis. Whether the alteration of the clause was made by the original scribe or by some other hand, we are not expert enough to be able to give an opinion. But what we have said is, we think, enough to make us hesitate in accepting the clause as it stands as being the original words of the Codex, with the omitted ὤν inserted.

Of the other uncials enumerated by Scrivener, C is regarded by experts as belonging to the fifth century, E and Λ to the seventh or eighth, the rest to the ninth or tenth. It is clear, therefore, that these manuscripts do not carry with them overwhelming weight on the score of antiquity. The cursives are not enumerated, but they can hardly claim greater authority than the uncials.

Then it would be easy to overestimate the testimony of the ecclesiastical writers referred to. Many of them, no doubt, never troubled themselves about critical questions. Finding the clause as a current gloss in the Churches in early times, many might introduce it into their sermons and writings without looking very carefully to see whether it was in their manuscript or not. There are similar glosses current in the present day, and we can well believe that many who use them, if sitting down to write, would transfer them to their pages, in the belief that they were genuine Scripture. This was far more likely to happen in primitive times, when there were few facilities for reference. Griesbach warns us against placing too much reliance upon the remains of Origen which have come down to us. We cannot be sure that the Latin of Rufinus is correct, and Griesbach says that the copies from which Origen quoted were not always reliable. As to Cyril of Alexandria, Westcott and Hort charge Aubert, his editor, with inserting the clause in question into the text which he printed in 1638; and they add that this is not the only instance in which Aubert has taken liberties with his author. If anyone will take the trouble to turn up Cyril's Commentary on John, in *The Library of the Fathers*, at ch. iii. 13, he will find that, while the clause is printed in the text, not a word is said of it in the exposition. It is impossible to resist the conclusion that the words were not before Cyril when he wrote his Commentary, and that Aubert must have inserted them on his own authority. Subsequent editors have copied Aubert slavishly. Then it seems hardly fair to mention Nonnus as an authority on such a question. A metrical paraphrase of John's Gospel in Greek by him is the source of this reading. Burgon was too much of a partisan to be followed with implicit trust.

Scrivener attempts to defend the clause by appealing to the critical rule, that the more difficult reading is to be preferred to the simpler one. But this rule cannot apply here. He says the clause is doubtless difficult; but where is the simpler reading which any one proposes to substitute for it? The question really is between this reading and none at all. No critic in modern times, so far as we are aware, dreams of accepting either of the readings which we have classified as (3) and (4).

Alford appeals, in support of the clause, to ch. i. 18, "The only-begotten Son, which is in the bosom of the Father, He hath declared Him." We fail to see the appropriateness of the appeal. John speaks there of the ascended Christ. He has gone back into the bosom of the Father—$\epsilon\dot{\iota}\varsigma\ \tau\grave{o}\nu\ \kappa\acute{o}\lambda\pi o\nu\ \tau o\hat{v}\ \Pi\alpha\tau\rho\acute{o}\varsigma$. The phrase is a pregnant one. In this passage with which we are now dealing Christ is speaking of Himself as still on earth. There is no parallel between the two passages.

II. The evidence against the clause is given with considerable fulness by Westcott and Hort. Of the uncials they specify ℵ, B, L, $T_b$; of the cursives they can adduce only number 33, which, however, has earned the honourable distinction of being called "queen of the cursives."[1] Of versions they mention the Memphitic and the best Æthiopic Codex. Of ecclesiastical writers they name Cyril of Alexandria's Commentary on the passage, referred to above.

A second branch of the evidence adduced by Westcott and Hort consists of proof of their statement that many quotations of ver. 13 stop short at τοῦ ἀνθρώπου, and that it is morally certain that most of them would have included ὁ ὢν ἐν τῷ οὐρανῷ if it had stood in the copies which the writers used.[2] They instance Origen on Proverbs, 110 of Tischendorf's edition; the Latin fragment by the same writer on Isaiah, and Eusebius, in two places. (Tischendorf tells us these references are to the work on Psalms, 403, and to the *Ecclesiastical History*, 82.) They refer to Adamant in Origen's *Works*, i. 855. (Is not Adamant another name for Origen himself?) They mention also *The Heresies* of Epiphanius, 487, 911. Gregory of Nazianzen, both in his letter to Cledonius, 87, and in that to Nectarius, his successor in the see of Constantinople, 168; Didymus on the Acts, in Cramer's *Catenæ*, vol. iii. p. 41, Oxon. 1838, which we have verified. They give, in brackets, an alternative reference, " = 1657 Mi." (Does this mean some passage in Migne's *Patrologia Græca*?) Then they adduce Gregory of Nyssa, *Against the Apollinarians*, 6;

---

[1] Westcott and Hort say that C and D are defective here. Scrivener adds F to these.

[2] We here fill in the somewhat severe contractions of Westcott and Hort to the best of our ability. We cannot guarantee absolute, but only approximate, accuracy. Writing in the provinces, we have not had the facilities for reference which the contractions of Westcott and Hort require. We wish they had been a little more liberal with their information.

the spurious writings of Pope Julius of Rome, 119 lag. (? edited by Lagarde). We are told that there are thirteen places in Cyril's writings in which the clause would with moral certainty have been quoted[1] if Cyril had found it in the copy which he used. We are next invited, in brackets, to consult E. P. Pusey on Cyril's *Scholia de Incarnatione Unigeniti*, p. 128. Then we have Jerome on Eph. iv. 10; and, lastly, Ephraem Syrus, as represented by the Armenian translation of his Commentary on the *Diatessaron* of Tatian, 168, 187, 189.

It will hardly be denied by any fair reader that this furnishes a very powerful argument for the excision of the clause from the text, especially if we take into consideration the strong internal evidence which we have stated at the beginning of this paper. In the hands of a special pleader like Burgon, if he had held a brief for this side of the question, it would have been made to appear unanswerable. We attach all the more weight to this evidence when we think of the calm and dispassionate manner in which Westcott and Hort present it.

Scrivener and Burgon make attempts to discredit this evidence in a way which does not seem to us to do them much credit. Scrivener tries to damage the testimony of א, B, and L by saying that they read in ch. i. 18, $\mu o\nu o\gamma \epsilon\nu\grave{\eta}\varsigma\ \Theta\epsilon\acute{o}\varsigma$. This appeal to the *odium theologicum* seems strangely unworthy of so great a man. Burgon brands the five manuscripts which exclude the clause as of bad character. This cannot be called fair criticism, and we do not think the learned world will endorse this *ex parte* judgment.

---

[1] Westcott (*Speaker's Commentary* on John) refers us to Pusey's *Cyril*, vii. 1, Pref. p. xx.

If you condemn these five manuscripts as bad, where, we ask, are the good ones to be found? We think we have shown that A has been tampered with since leaving the hand of the original scribe. No expert has given evidence as to the time at which the clause was inserted in that Codex.

Burgon says, "Since we have *proved* that Origen and Didymus, Epiphanius and Cyril, Ambrose and Jerome *recognise* the words in dispute, of what possible textual significancy can it be if presently (because it is sufficient for their purpose) the same Fathers are observed to quote St. John iii. 13 no further than down to the words '*Son of man*'?" The answer to this is that they may be quoting loosely and recording a popular gloss in the one case, while in the other they are adhering to the words of the codex before them. Again, he says, "Origen, Eusebius, Proclus, Ephraem Syrus, Jerome, Marius, where they are only insisting on the doctrinal significancy of the earlier words, naturally end their quotation at this place." This argument will hardly hold water. The great reason given for the retention of the clause is its doctrinal significancy. Authors writing with a doctrinal object, if they had occasion to quote this 13th verse at all, would certainly have quoted the clause in question if it had stood in their copies. The climax of false argumentation is reached when Burgon says, "The two Gregories, writing against the Apollinarian heresy, of course quoted the verse no further than Apollinaris himself was accustomed (for his heresy) to adduce it." There was nothing in Apollinarianism to induce its author to omit the clause in question, if it had stood in the copy which he used. The conclusion seems indisputable that neither the Gregories nor Apollinaris knew anything of it.

The view which we have sought to support is that which Tischendorf accepted in his *Synopsis Evangelica*, published in 1864. He has since repudiated it—we think on very insufficient grounds. We are glad to find ourselves in the company of such competent judges as the late Professor Milligan and Westcott and Hort. After all that has been said, it seems plain that it is much easier to account for its insertion, if not written by John, than for its omission, if it really came from the pen of the sacred writer. Scrivener's concluding words, in his note on the passage, are an outrage on critical intelligence. He says that the manuscripts which exclude the clause are convicted " of the deliberate suppression of one of the most mysterious, yet one of the most glorious, glimpses afforded to us in Scripture of the Saviour on the side of His Proper Divinity."

# SELECTION FROM
# Oliphant Anderson & Ferrier's Publications.

Post 8vo, art canvas, price 1s. 6d.,

**David Hume.** By Henry Calderwood. Being Volume XX. of the "Famous Scots" Series.

Large crown 8vo, cloth extra, price 5s.,

**The Personal Ministry of the Son of Man.** Studies in the Saviour's Application of His own Teaching. By the Rev. James Jeffrey, M.A.

Large crown 8vo, cloth extra, gilt top, price 5s.,

**Palestine, The Glory of all Lands.** By the Rev. Archibald Sutherland, Perth.

Crown 8vo, cloth extra, price 5s.,

**The Presbyterian Church:** Its Worship, Functions, and Ministerial Orders. By the Rev. Alexander Wright, M.A.

Large crown 8vo, cloth extra, price 3s. 6d.,

**Leaders in Literature:** Emerson—Carlyle and Emerson: A Comparison—Lowell—George Eliot—Mrs. Browning—Robert Browning—Matthew Arnold—Herbert Spencer—John Ruskin. By P. Wilson, M.A.

Post 8vo, art linen, gilt top, price 3s. 6d. each,

**Bible Characters:** Adam to Achan.

**Bible Characters:** Gideon to Absalom.
By the Rev. Alexander Whyte, D.D.

Post 8vo, art canvas, price 1s. 6d.,

**Norman Macleod.** By John Wellwood. Being Volume XIV. of the "Famous Scots" Series.

Crown 8vo, cloth, price 5s.,

**Memorials of the United Presbyterian Hall** for 140 Years. By the Rev. P. Landreth.

Small crown 8vo, illustrated paper covers, 6d.; cloth, 1s.,

**Elder Logan's Story about the Kirks.** A Book for the Young. By John Strathesk, Author of "Bits from Blinkbonny."

Crown 8vo, cloth, price 2s. 6d. each,

**Life's Stages:** Their Duties and Opportunities.

**Life's Phases:** A Sequel to "Life's Stages."
By James Stark, D.D.

Large crown 8vo, cloth extra, price 5s.,

**For Days of Youth.** A Bible Text and Talk for every Day of the Year. By the Rev. Charles A. Salmond, M.A.

Large crown 8vo, cloth extra, price 5s.,

**The Holy Spirit, The Paraclete.** By the Rev. John Robson, D.D.

**Selection from Oliphant Anderson & Ferrier's Publications**—*continued*.

Crown 8vo, cloth extra,, price 2s. 6d.,
## Plymouth Brethrenism Unveiled and Refuted.
By the Rev. William Reid, D.D. Third Edition.

Large crown 8vo, cloth extra, with Portrait, price 2s.,
## Pardon and Assurance.
By the Rev. William J. Patton. Edited, with a Biographical Sketch, by the Rev. John M'Ilveen, B.A. Fourth Edition.

Crown 8vo, cloth extra, price 3s. 6d.,
## What and How to Preach:
Being Lectures delivered in the College of the United Presbyterian Church. By the Rev. Alexander Oliver, D.D.

Post 8vo, cloth extra, price 2s. 6d.,
## Week-Day Religion.
By the Rev. J. R. Miller, D.D.

Crown 8vo, cloth extra, price 5s. each,
## The Gospel and Modern Substitutes.
## The Church and Social Problems.
Second Edition. By the Rev. A. Scott Matheson, Dumbarton.

Crown 8vo, cloth extra, price 7s. 6d.,
## Lectures, Exegetical and Practical, on the
Epistle of James. By the Rev. R. Johnstone, D.D. Second Ed.

Large crown 8vo, cloth extra, gilt top, price 5s.,
## Messages to the Children.
By the Rev. Charles Jerdan, Greenock.

Post 8vo, art canvas, price 1s. 6d.,
## John Knox.
By A. Taylor Innes. Being Volume IV. of the "Famous Scots" Series.

Large crown 8vo, cloth extra, with Map and Illustrations, price 5s.,
## Calabar and its Mission.
By the Rev. Hugh Goldie.

Post 8vo, art vellum, price 2s. 6d.,
## God's Measure, and other Sermons.
By the Rev. J. T. Forbes, M.A.

Post 8vo, cloth extra, price 1s. 6d.,
## Silver Wings, and other Addresses to Children.
By Andrew G. Fleming.

Post 8vo, cloth extra, price 1s. 6d.,
## A Bag with Holes, and other Addresses to Children
By the Rev. James Aitchison, Falkirk.

Demy 8vo, cloth, with Portrait, price 2s.,
## Life of the Rev. Henry Belfrage, D.D., of
Falkirk. By the Rev. John M'Kerrow and the Rev. John M'Farlane.

www.ingramcontent.com/pod-product-compliance
Lightning Source LLC
Chambersburg PA
CBHW021844230426
43669CB00008B/1076